MW00887562

THIS BOOK BELONGS TO :

- -

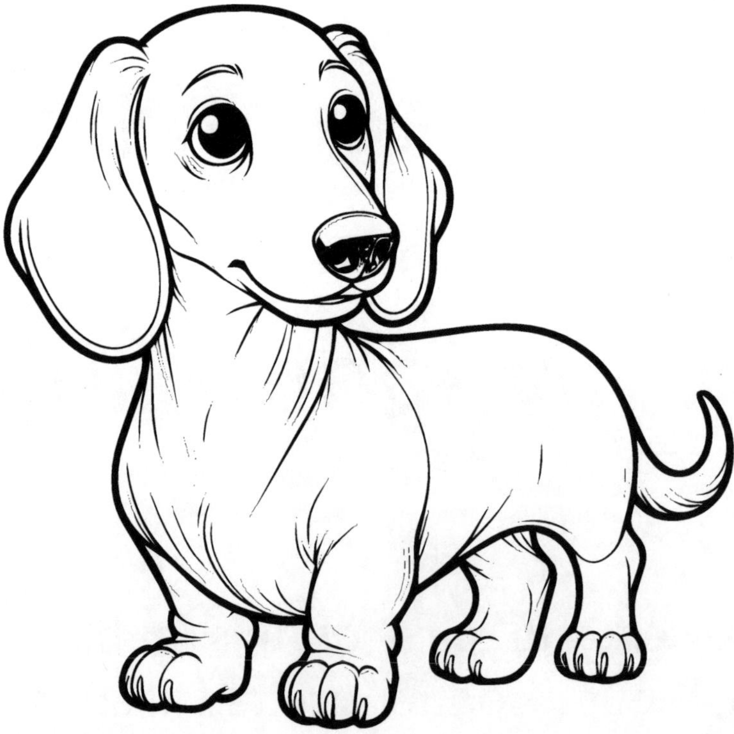

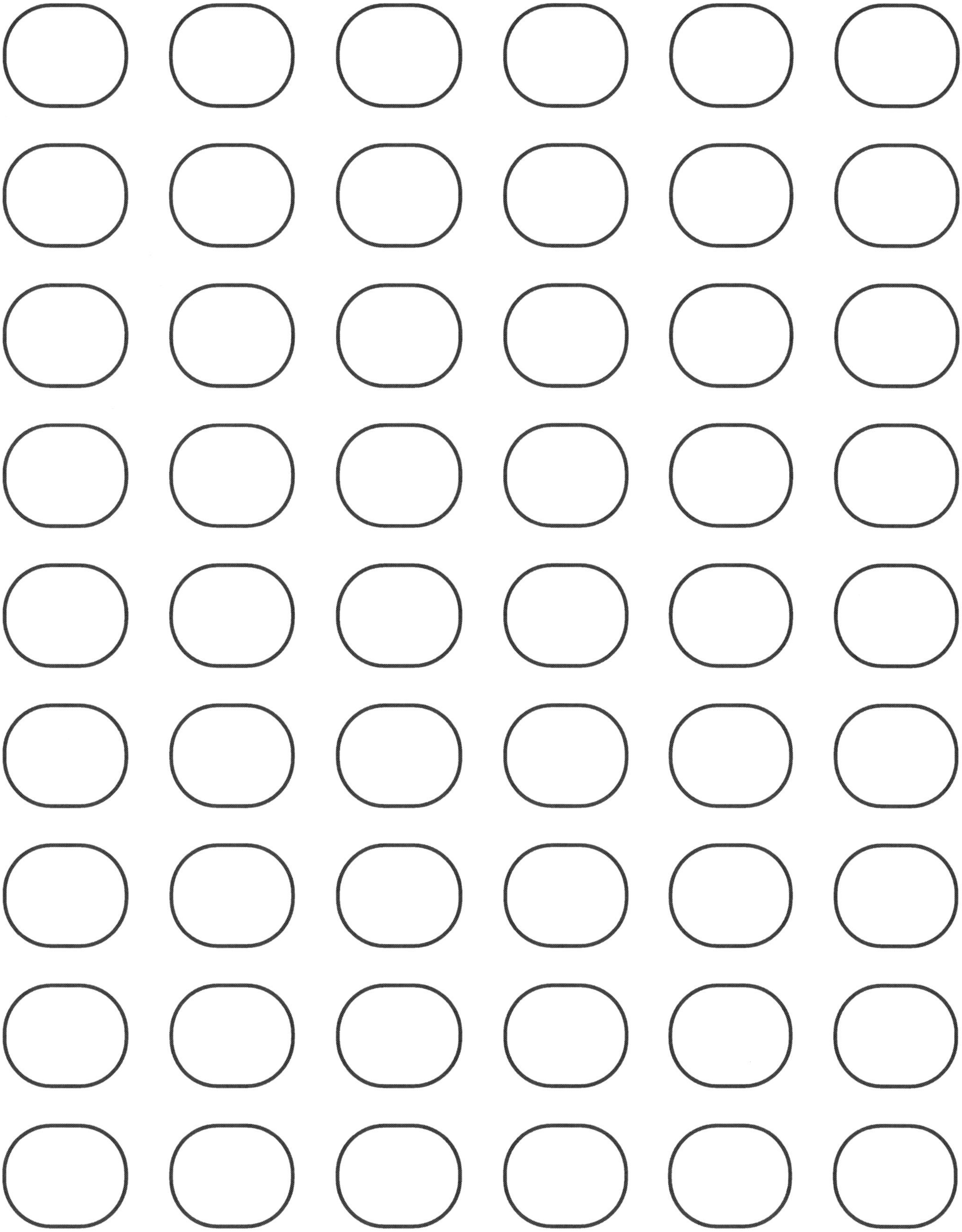

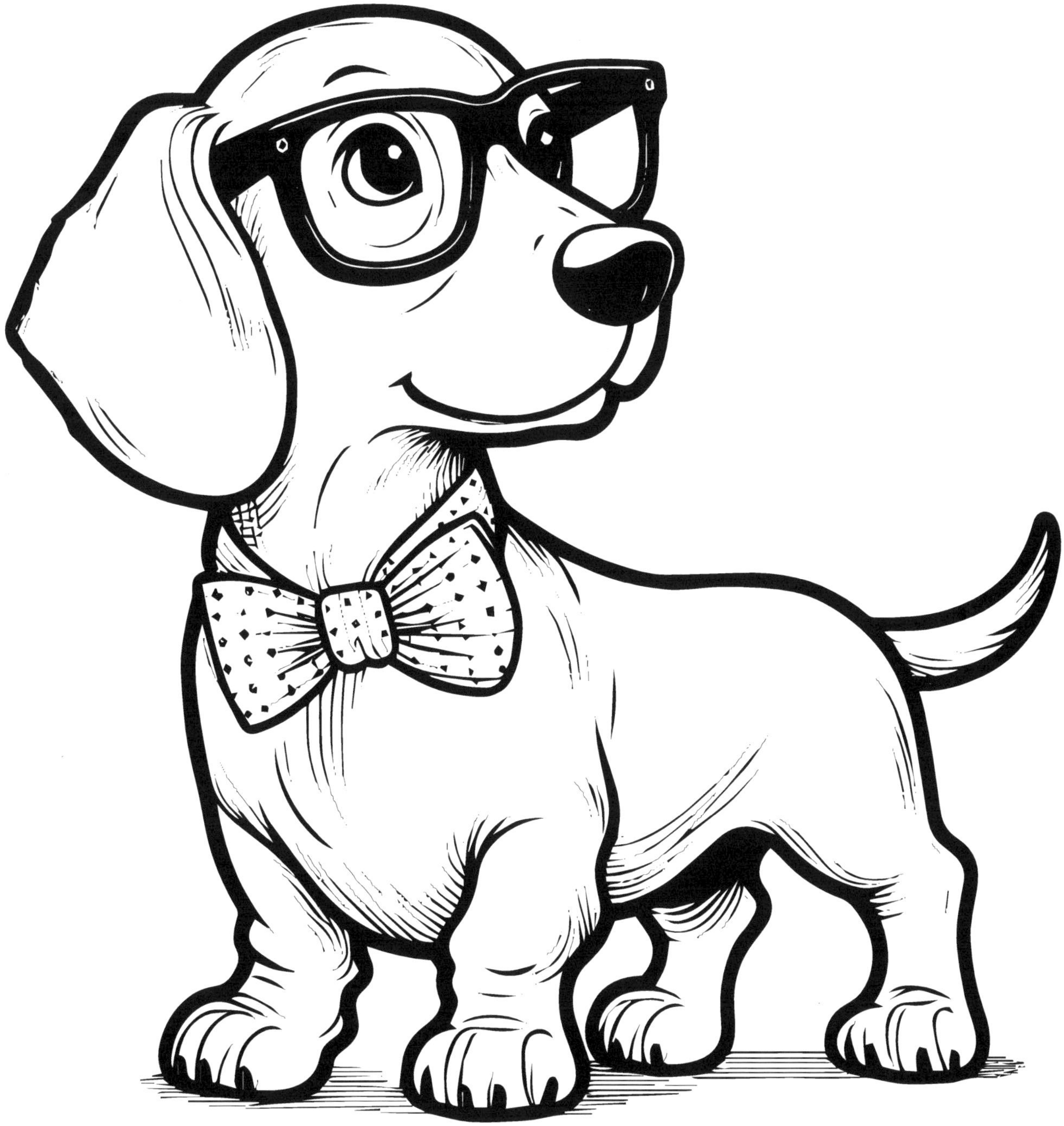

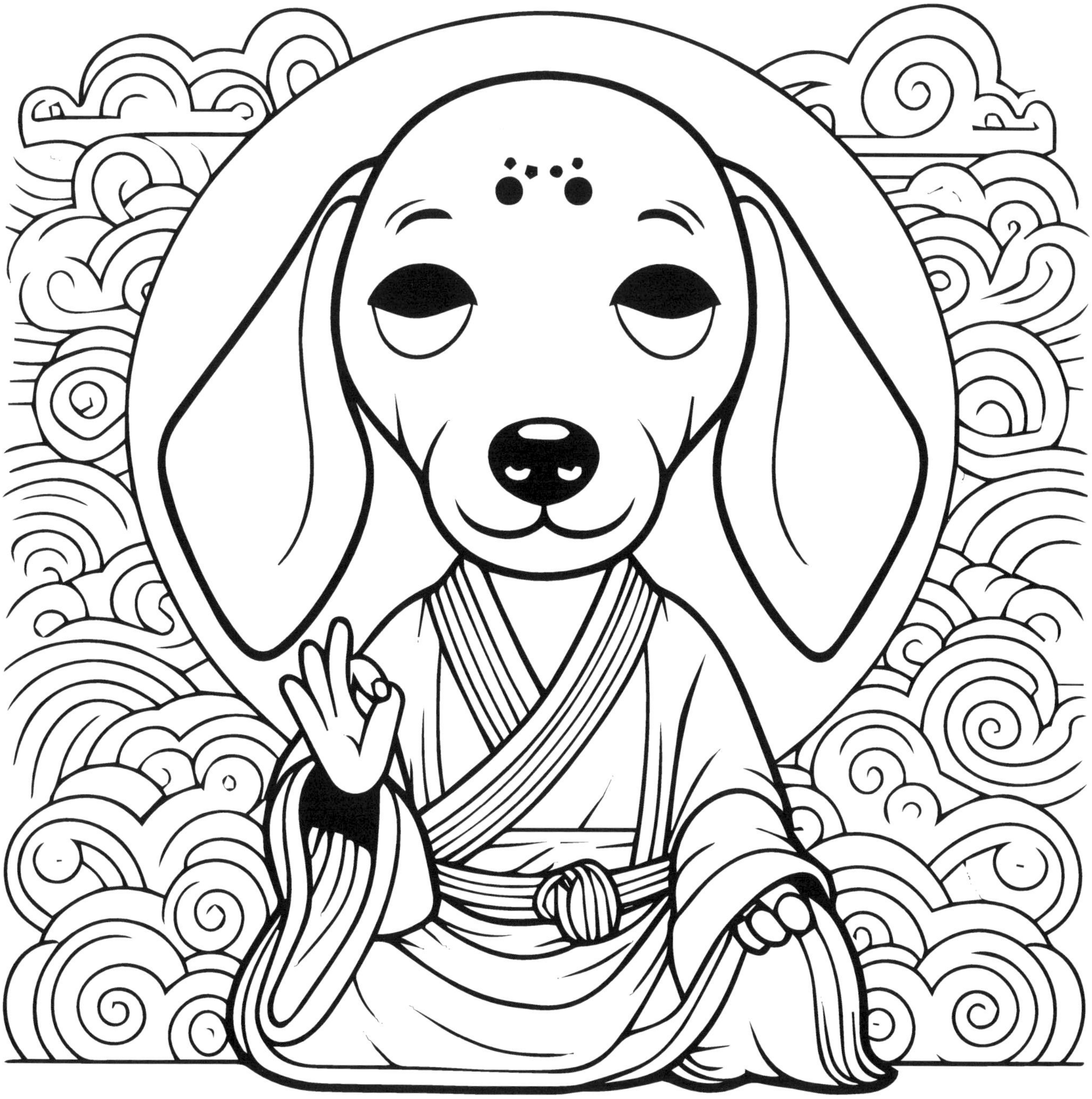

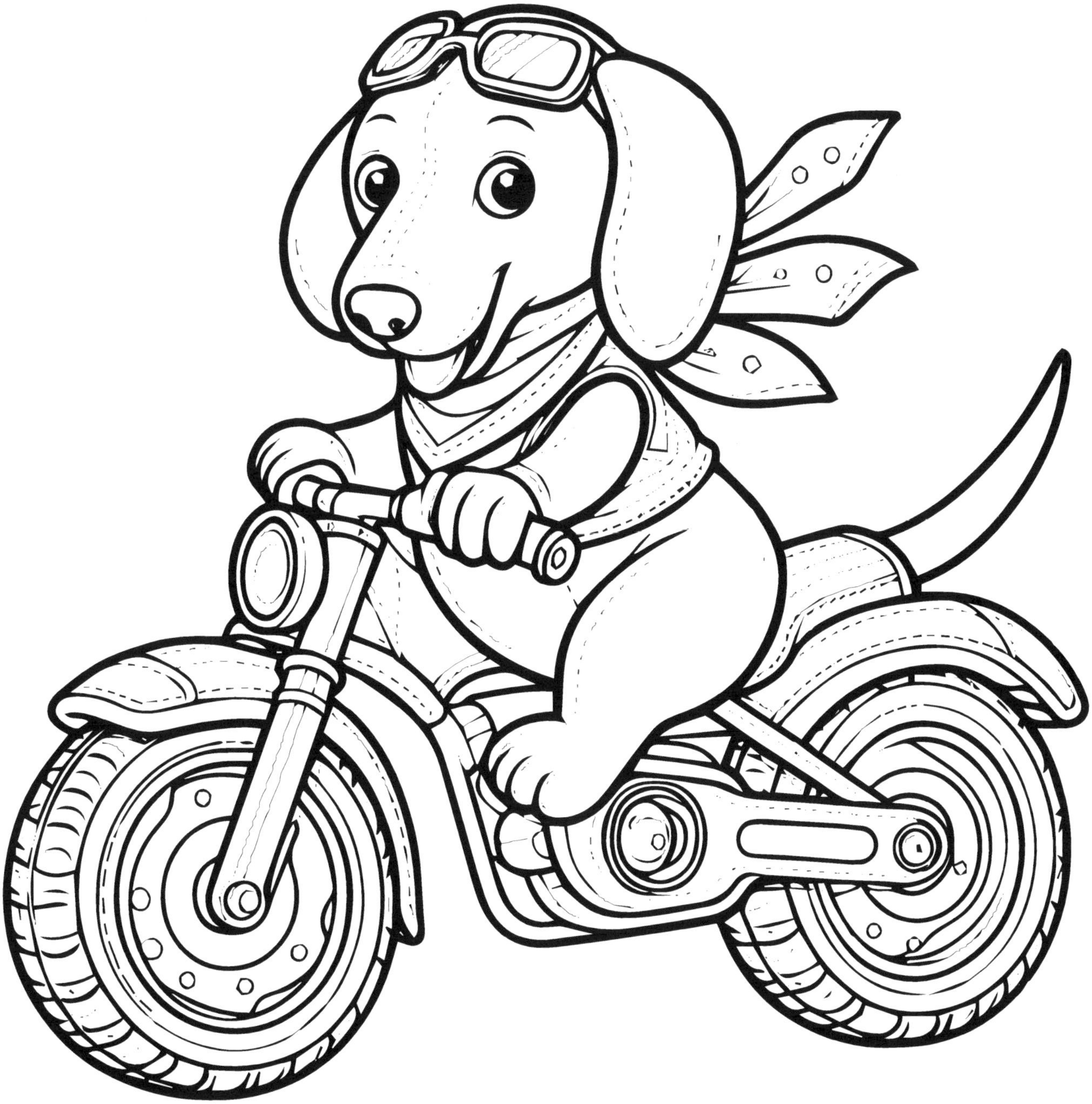

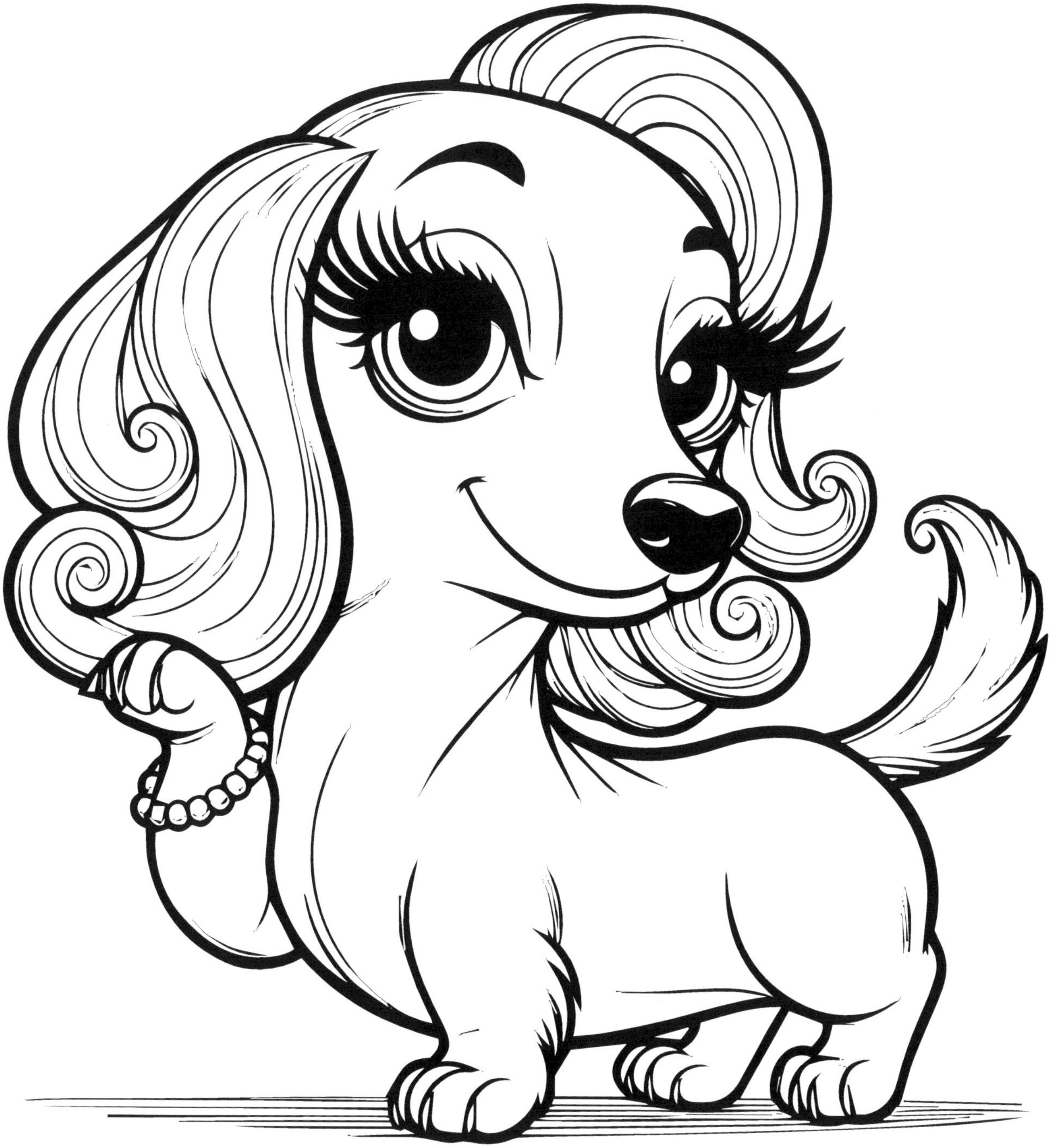

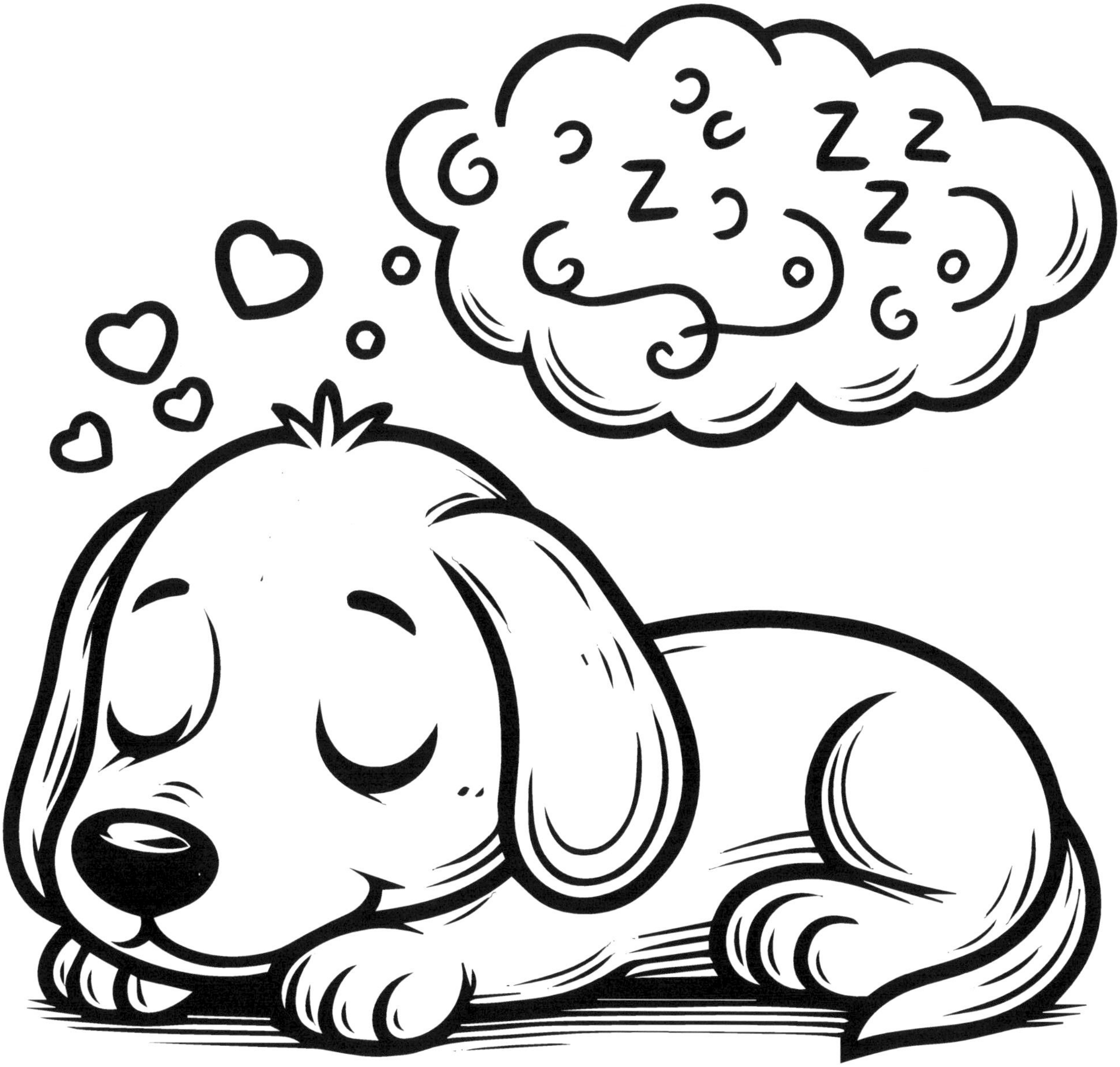

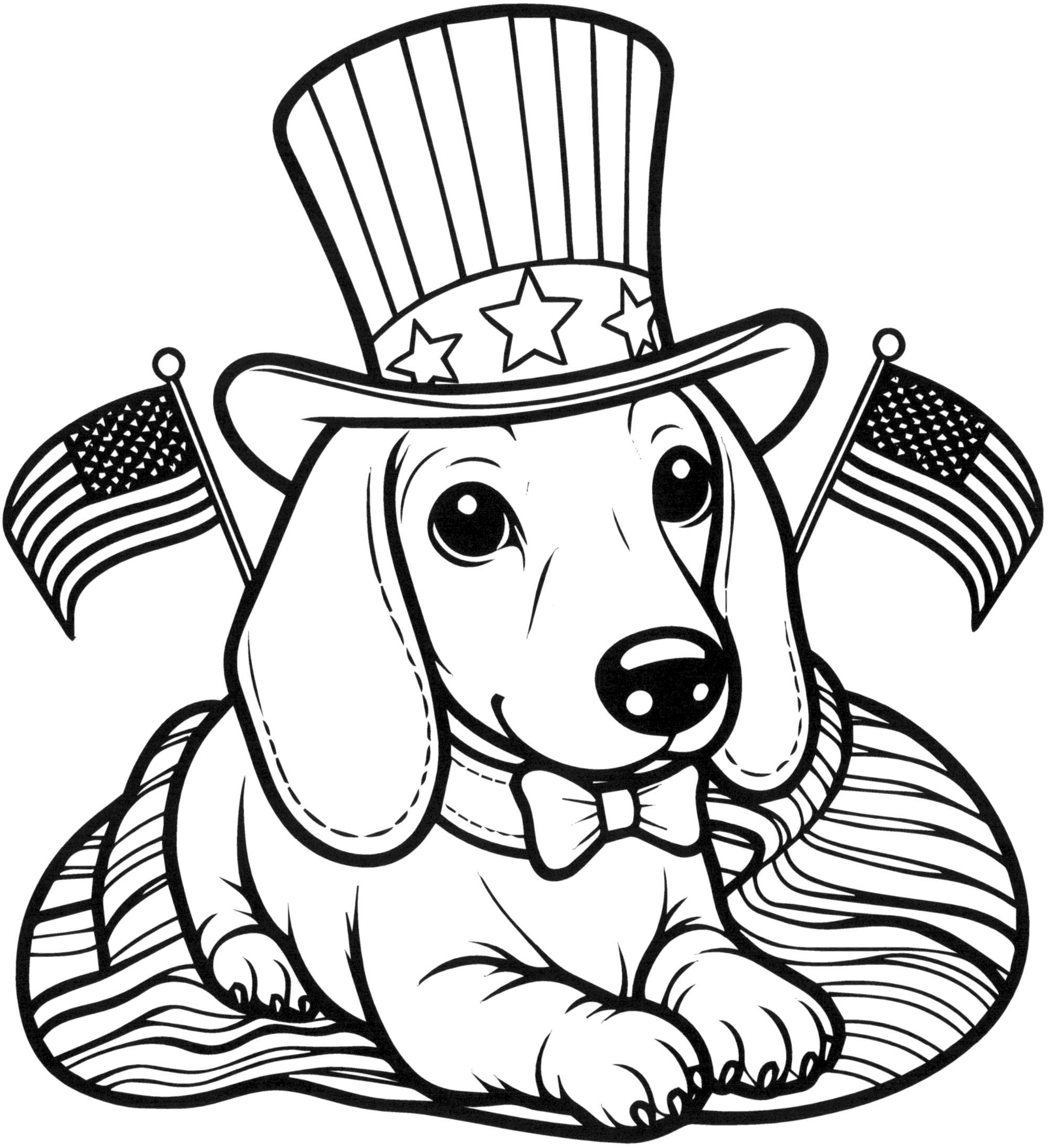

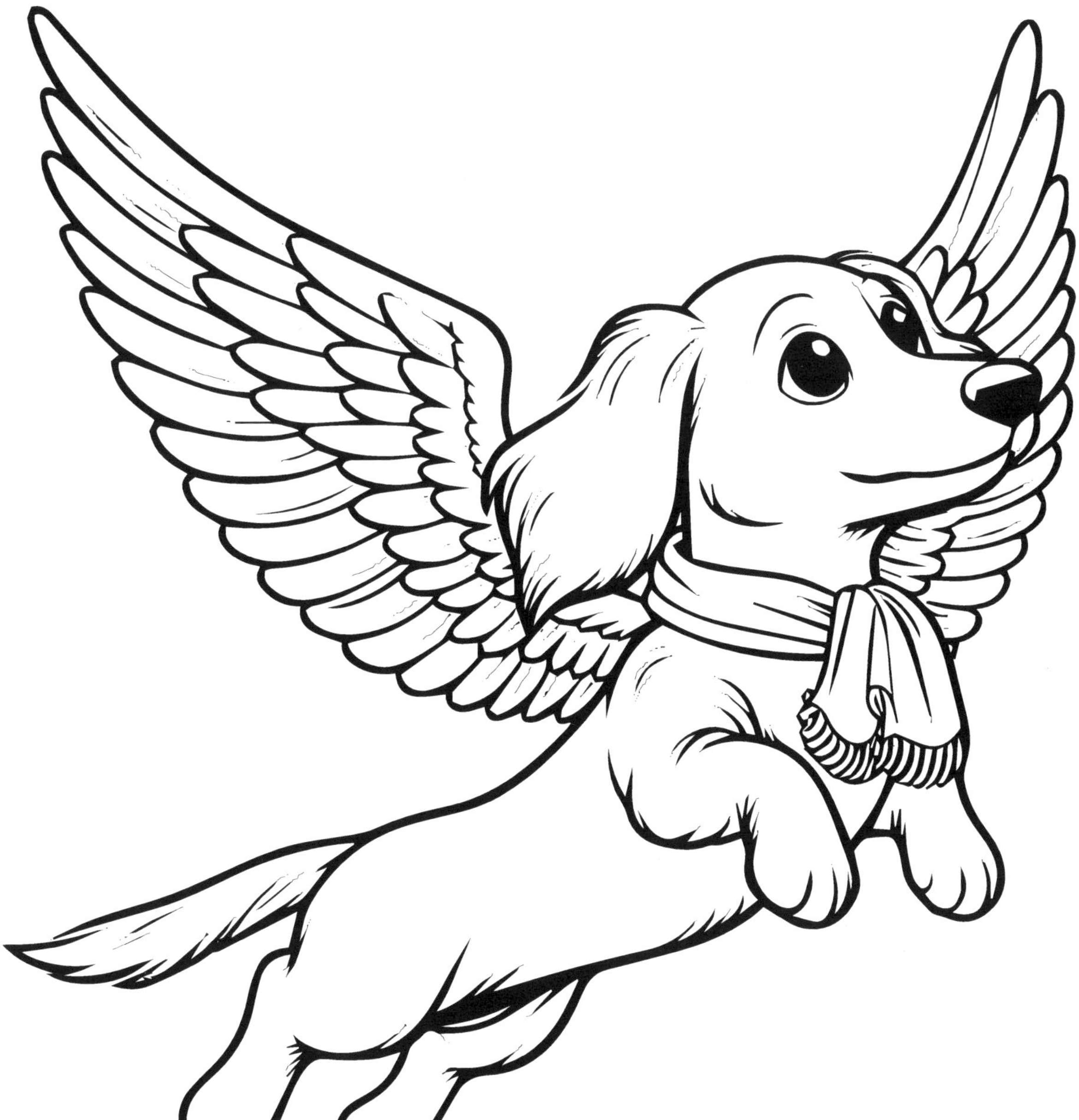

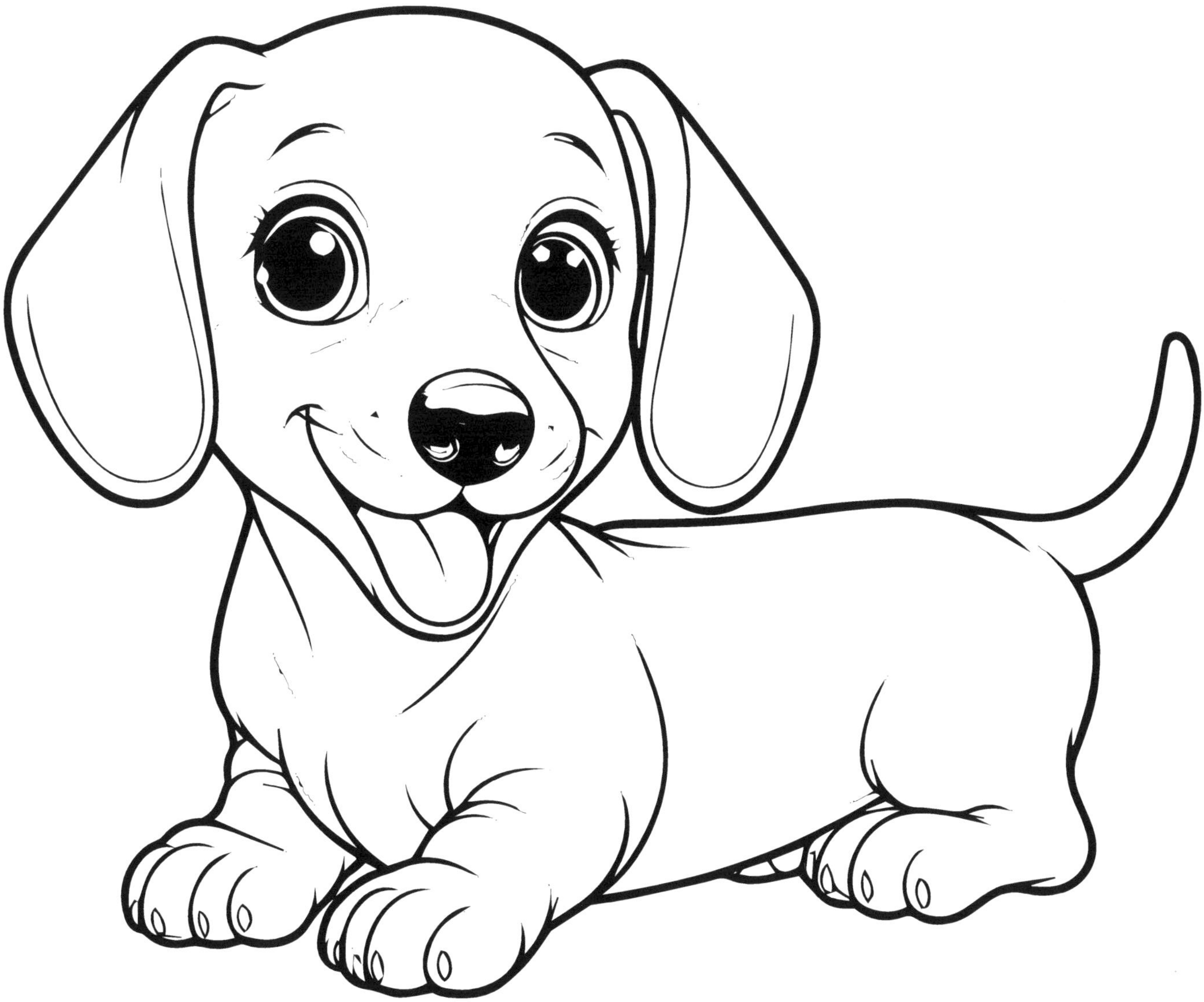

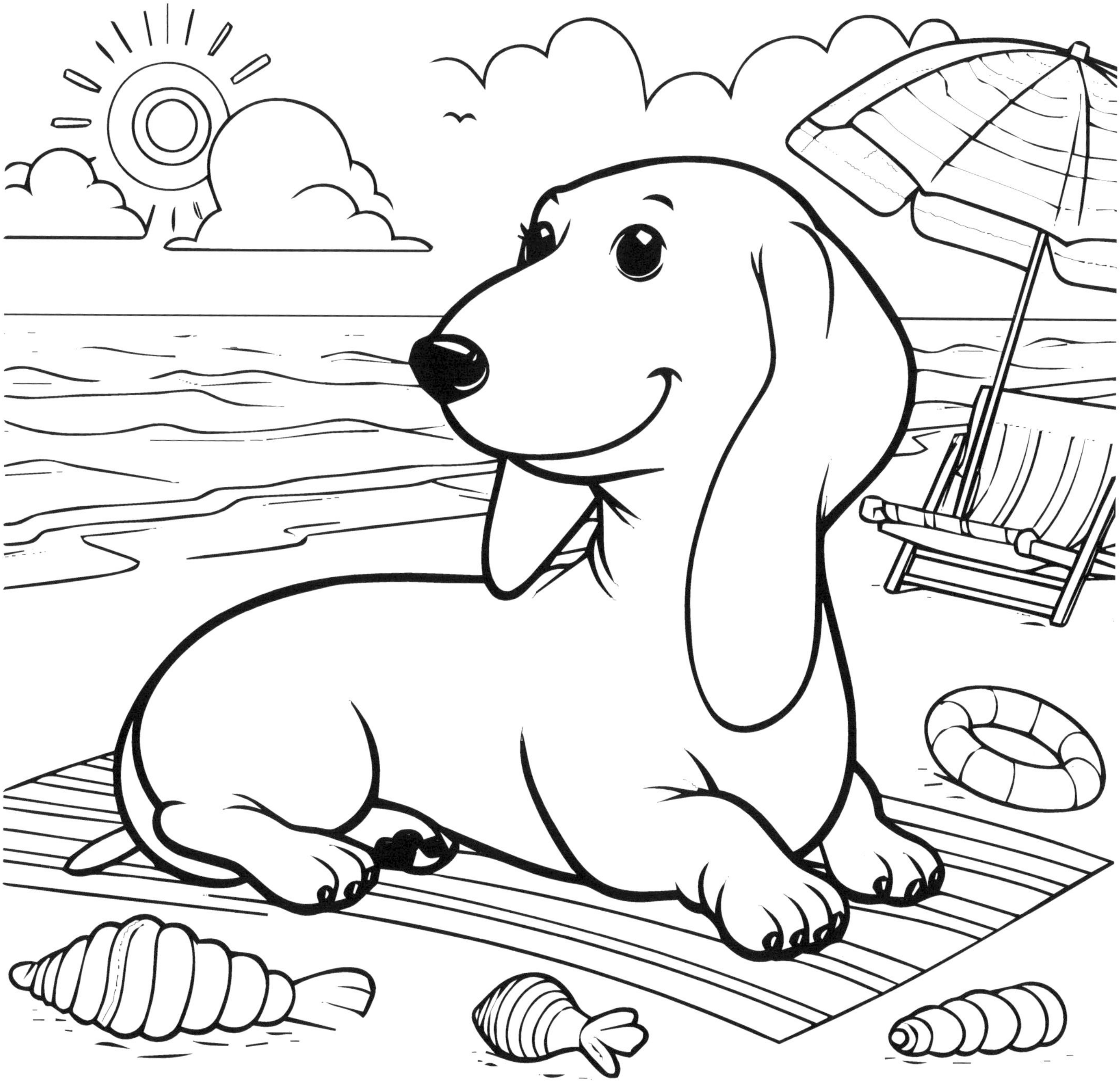

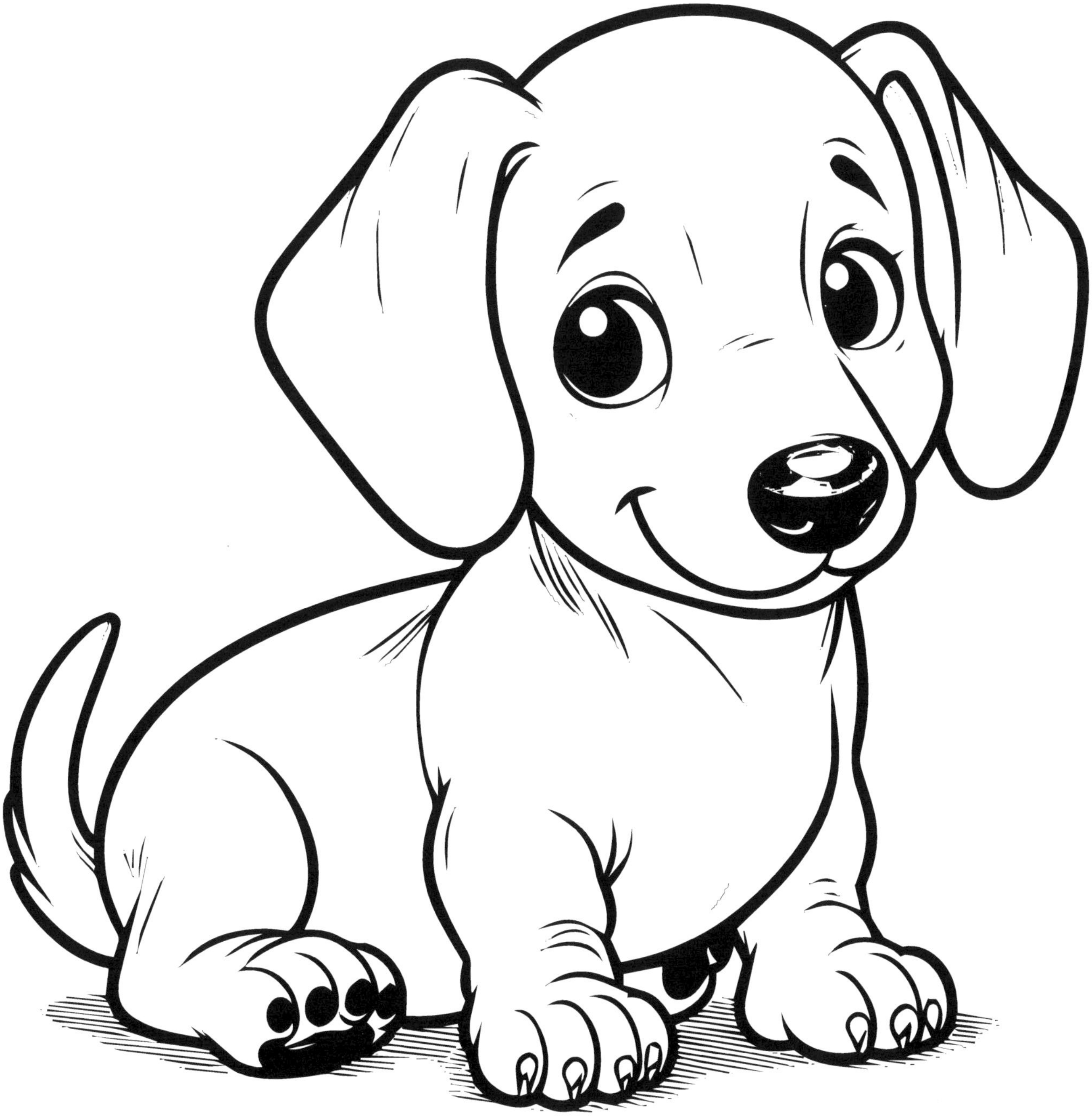

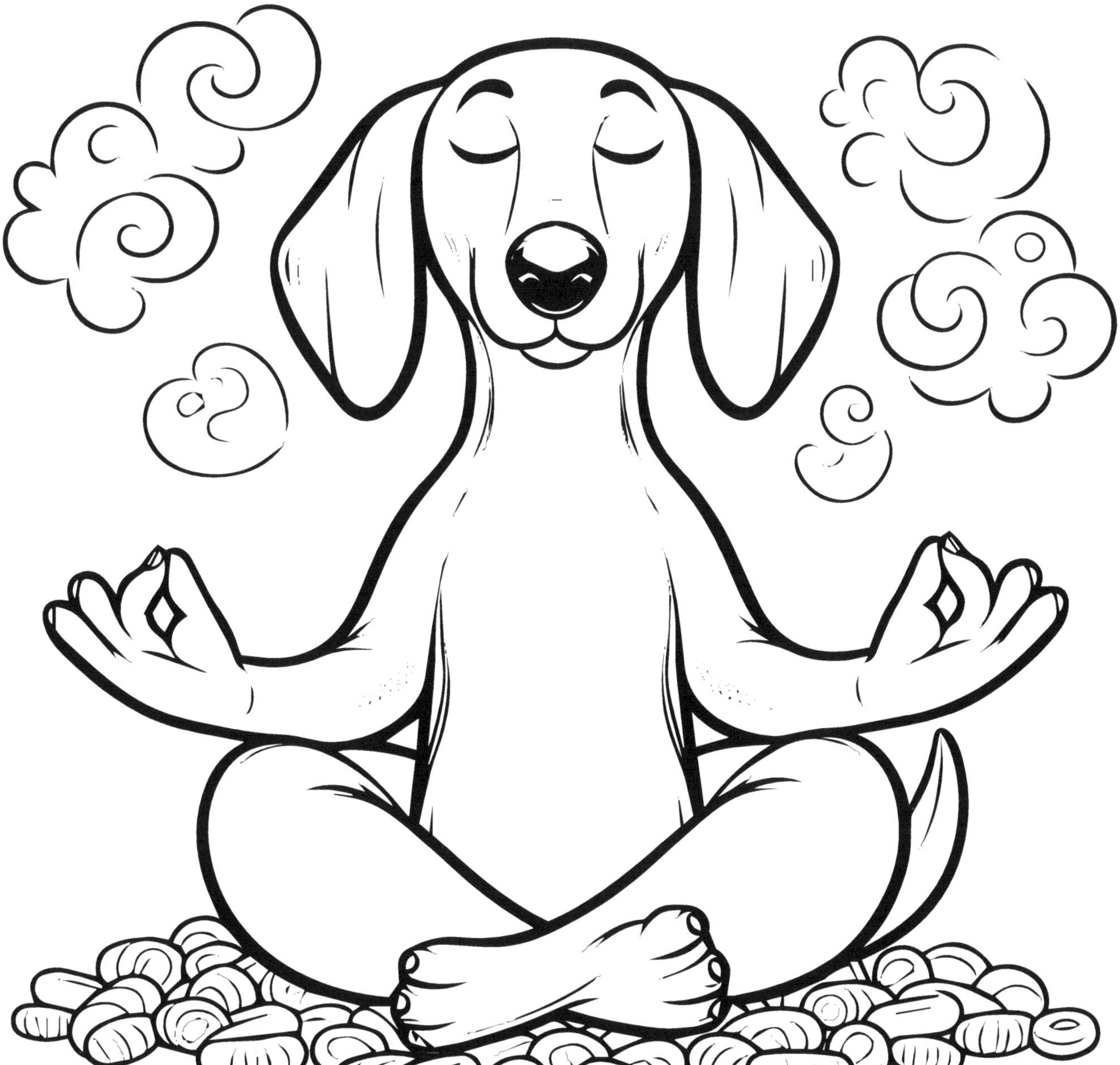

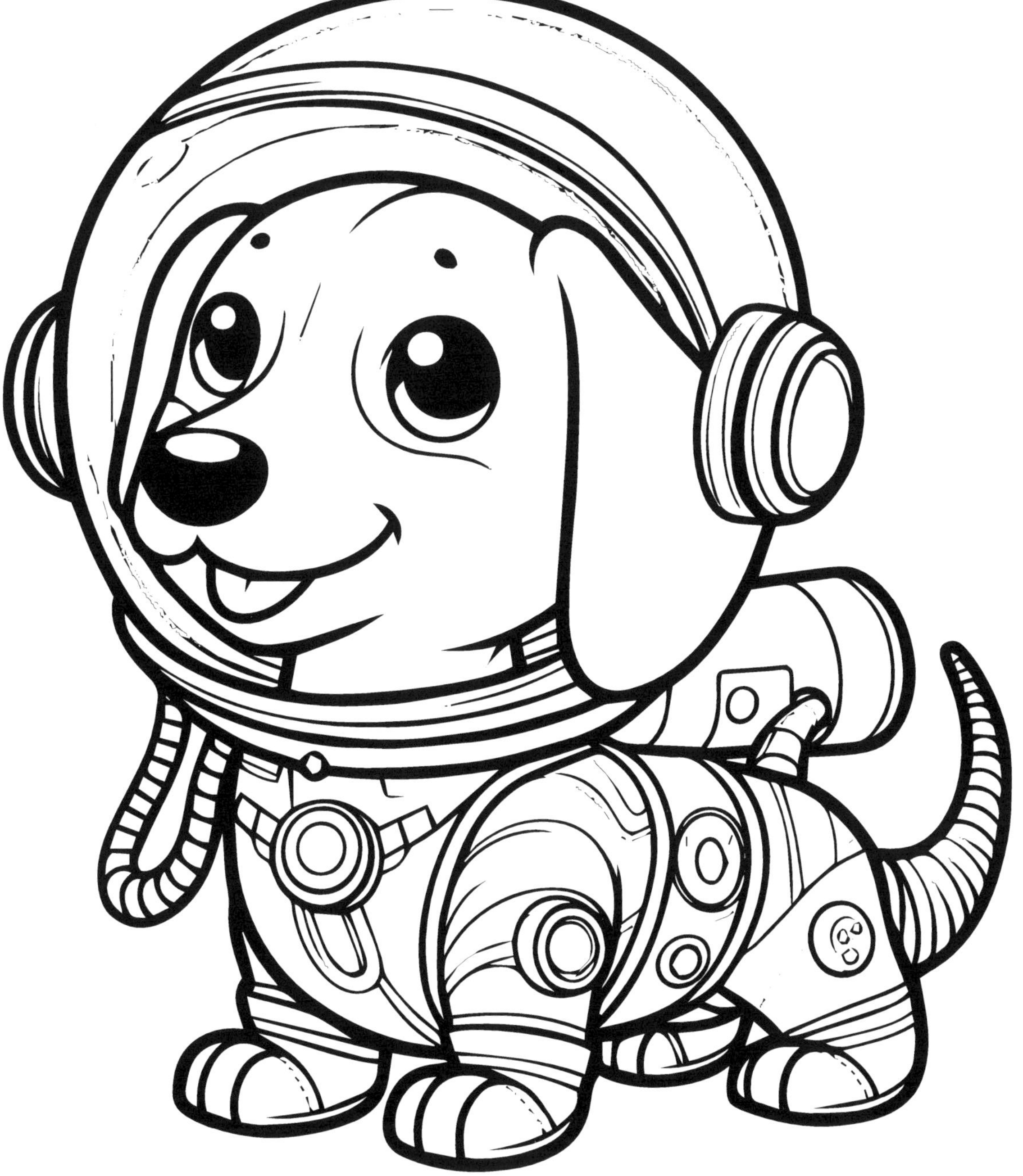

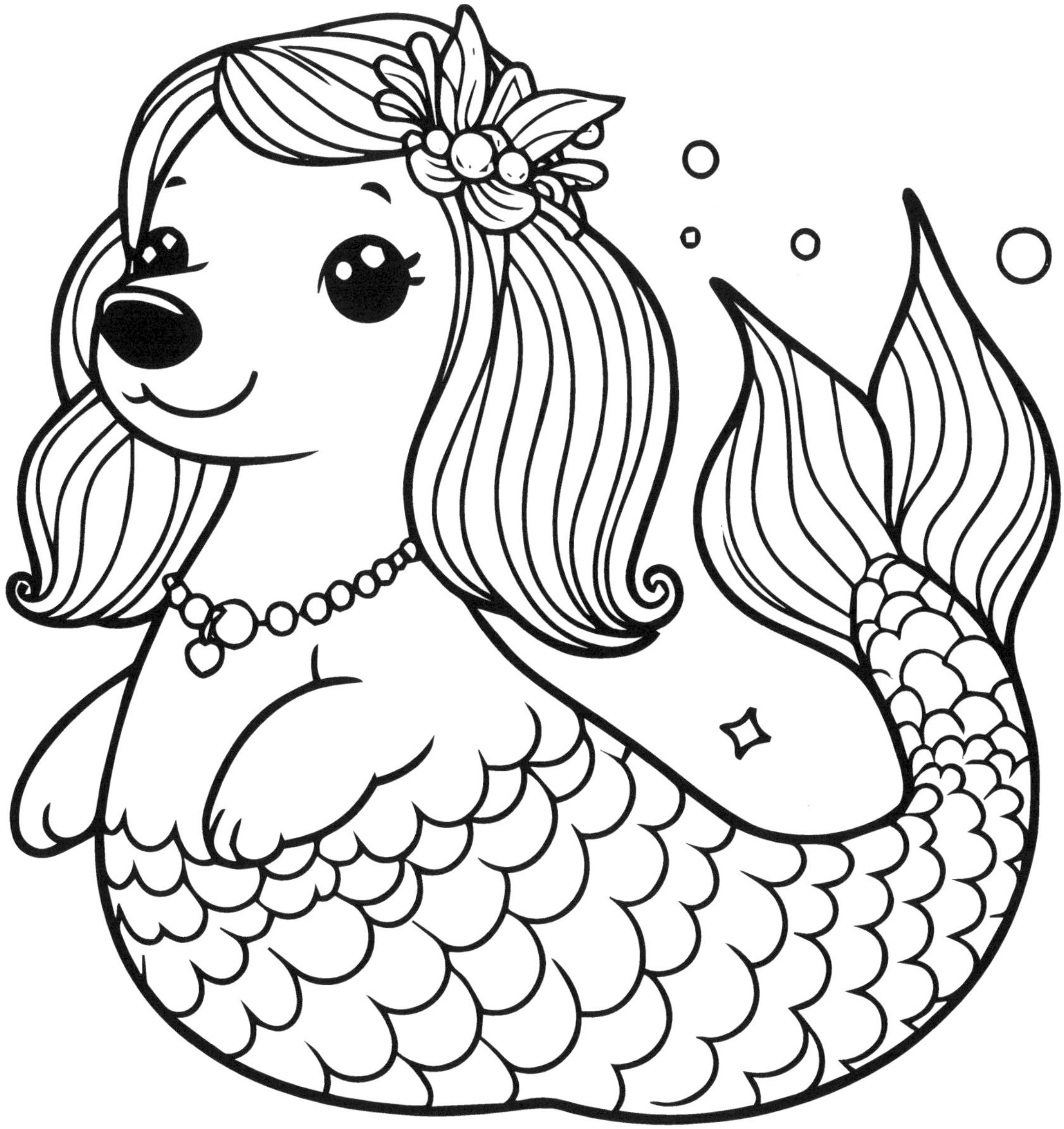

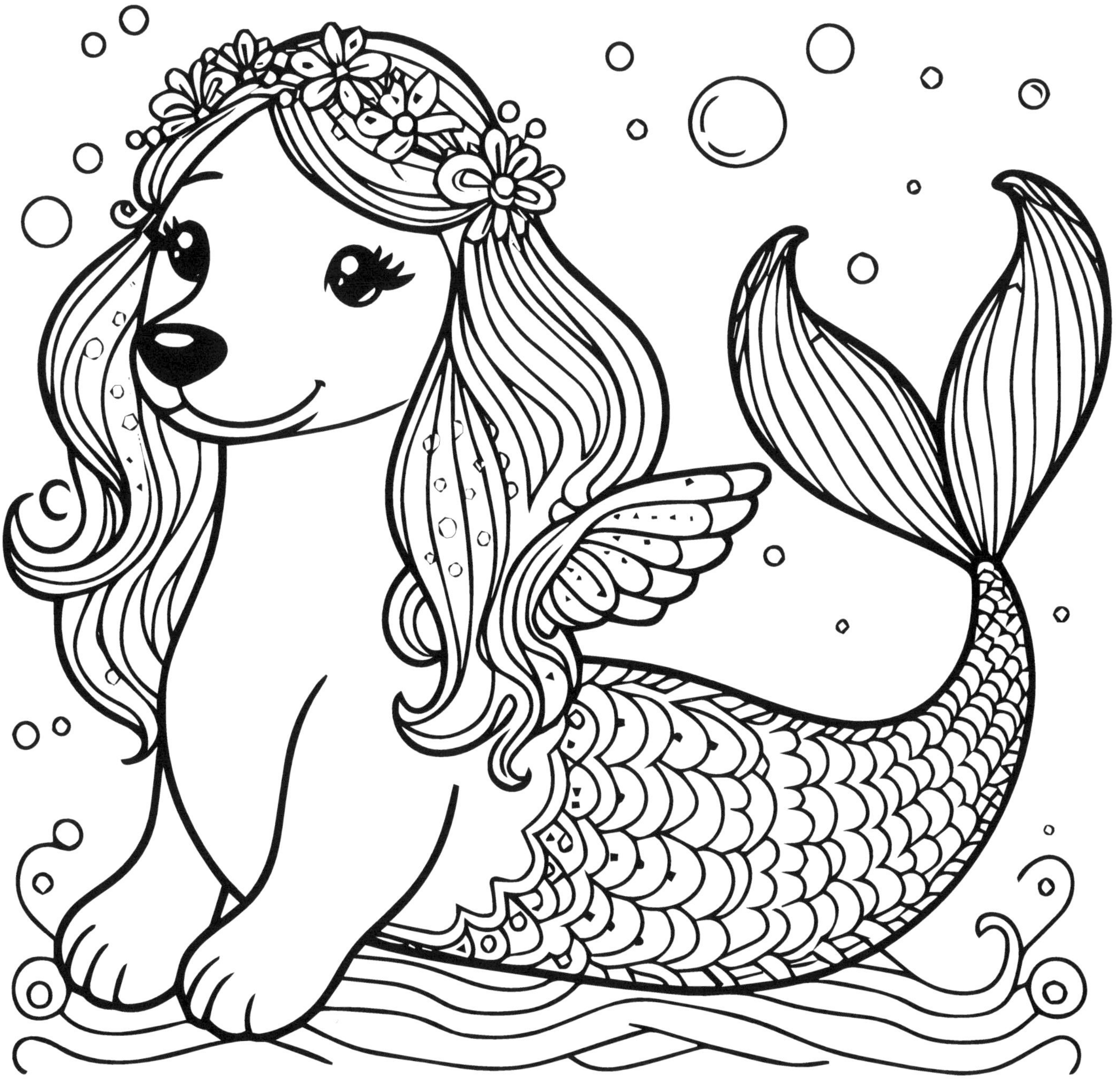

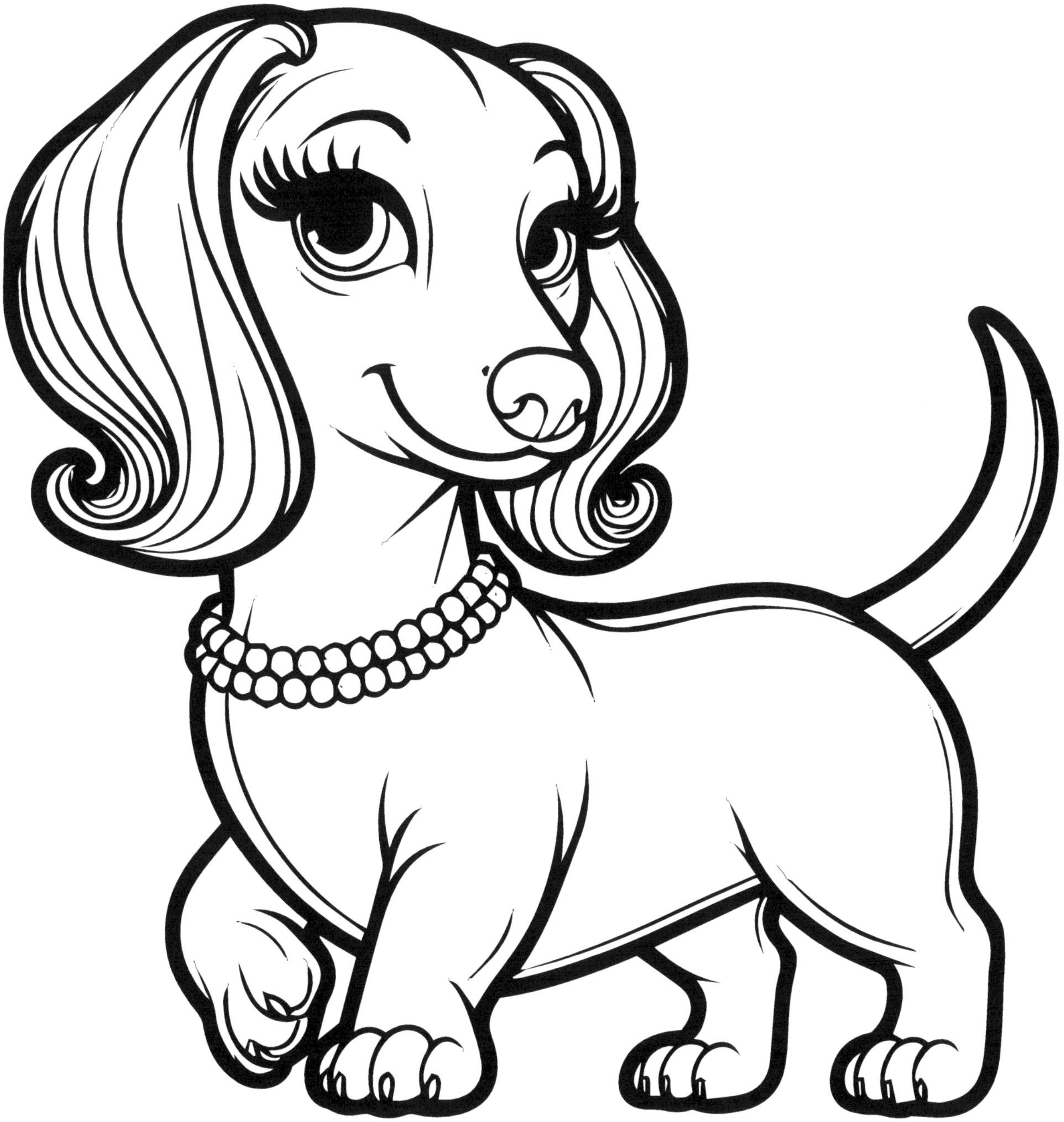

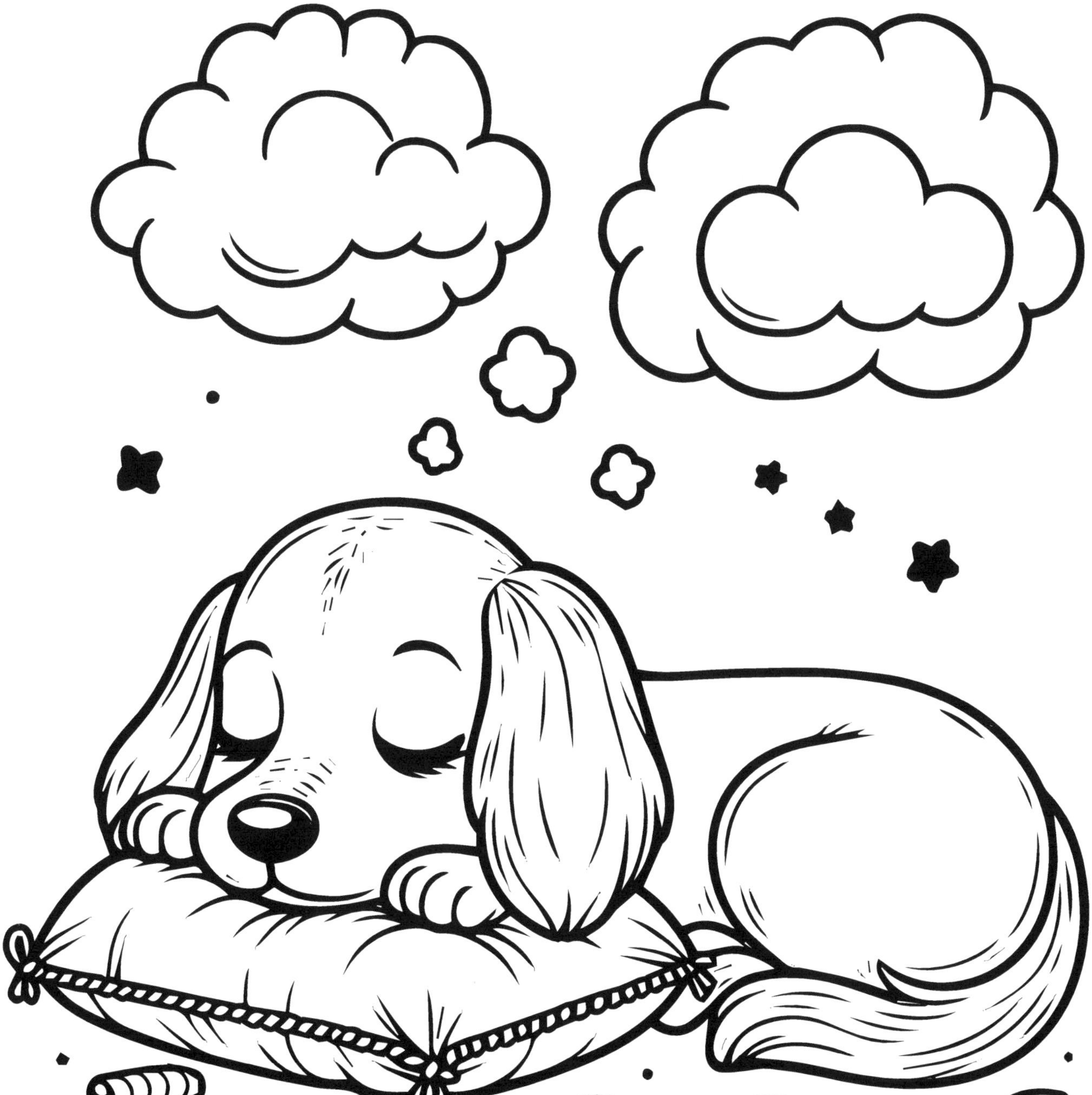

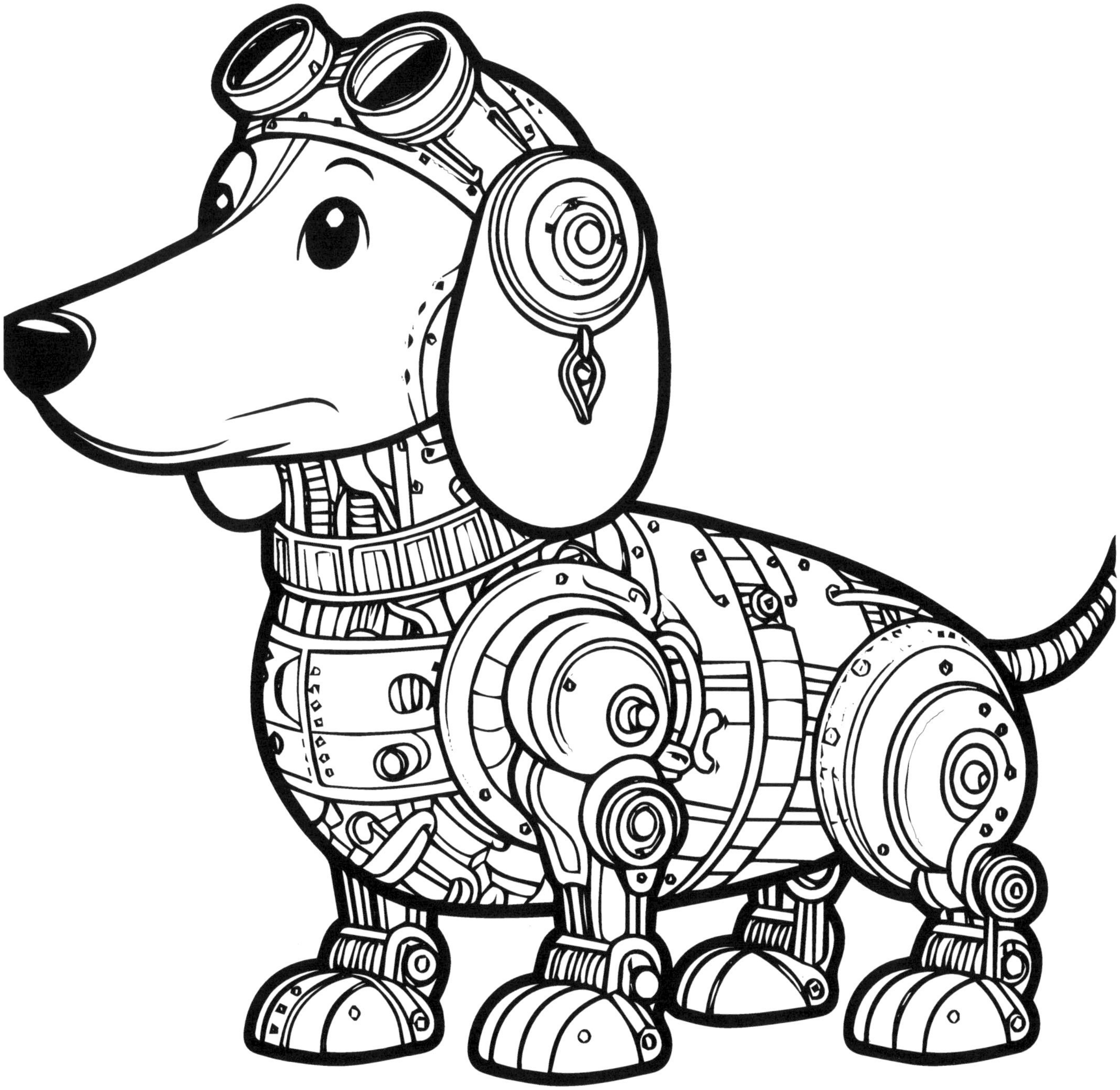

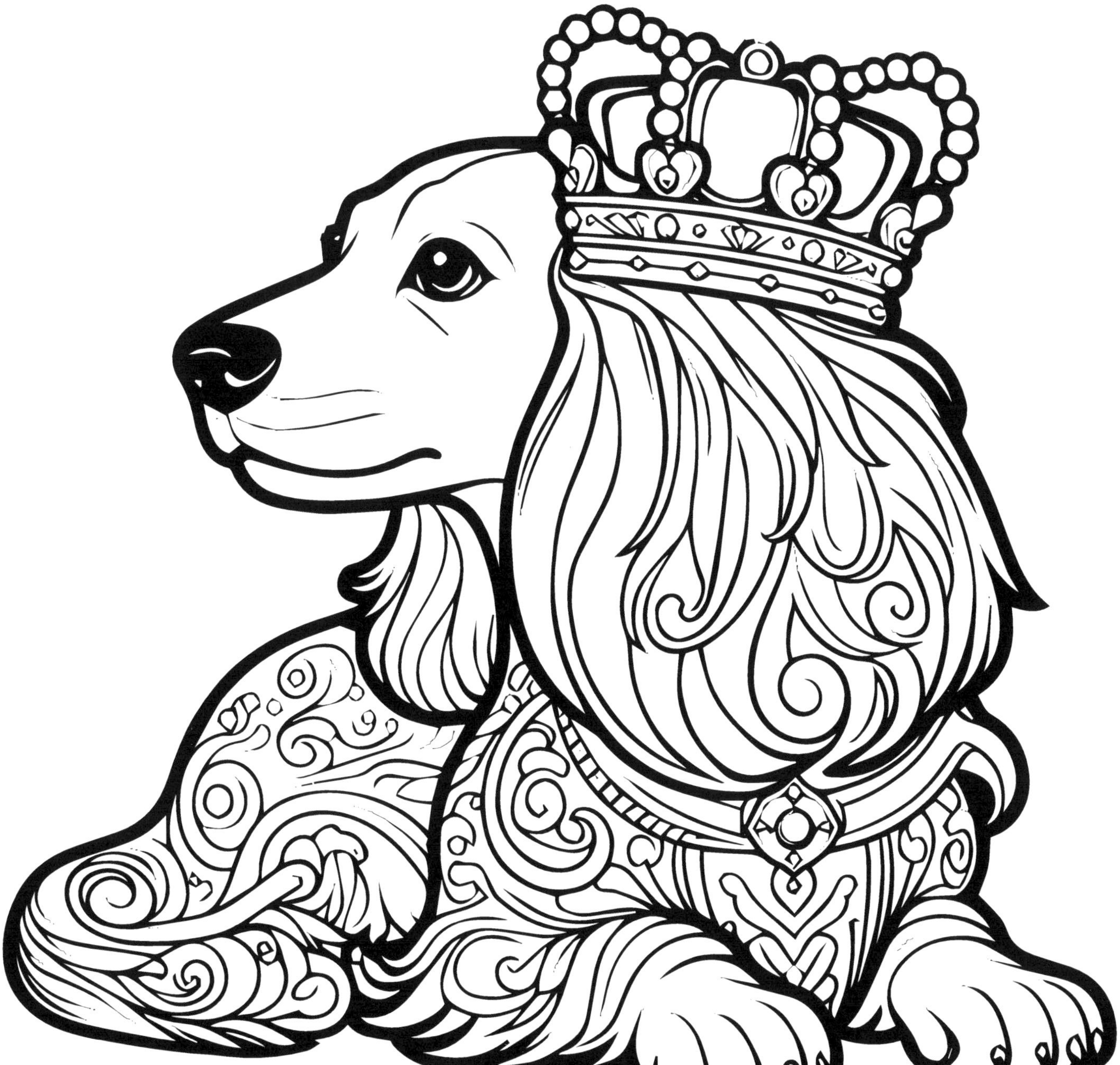

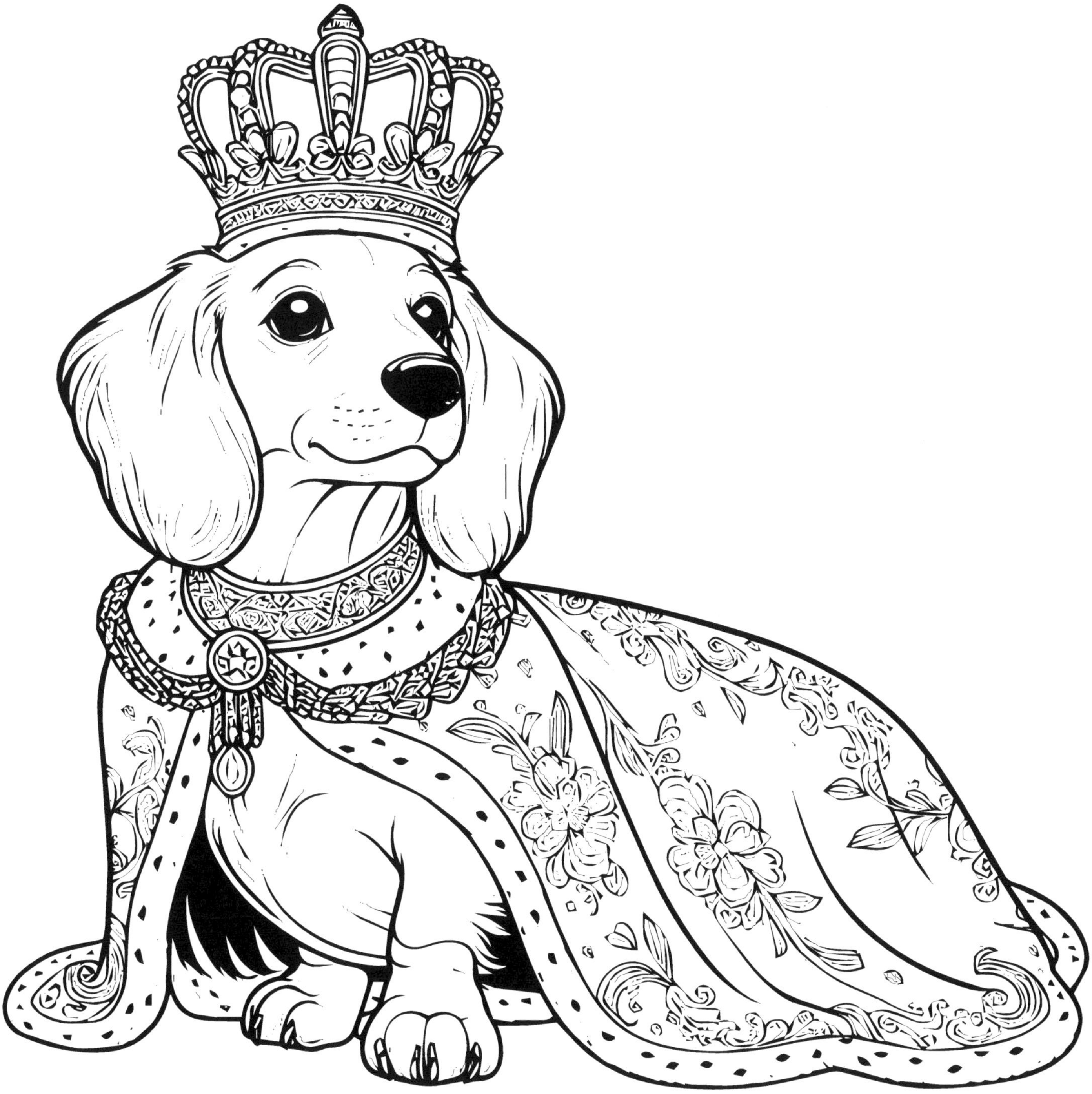

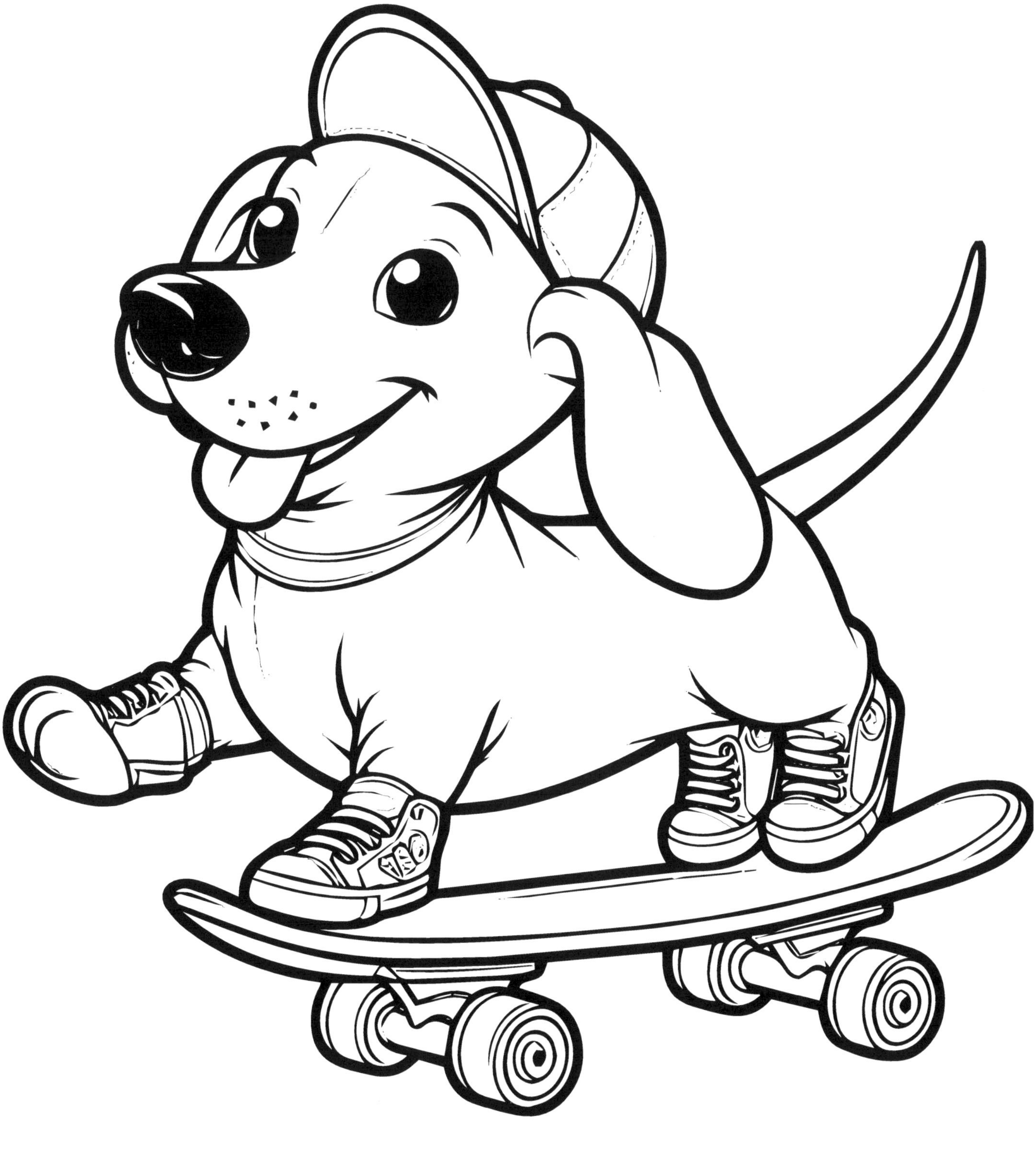

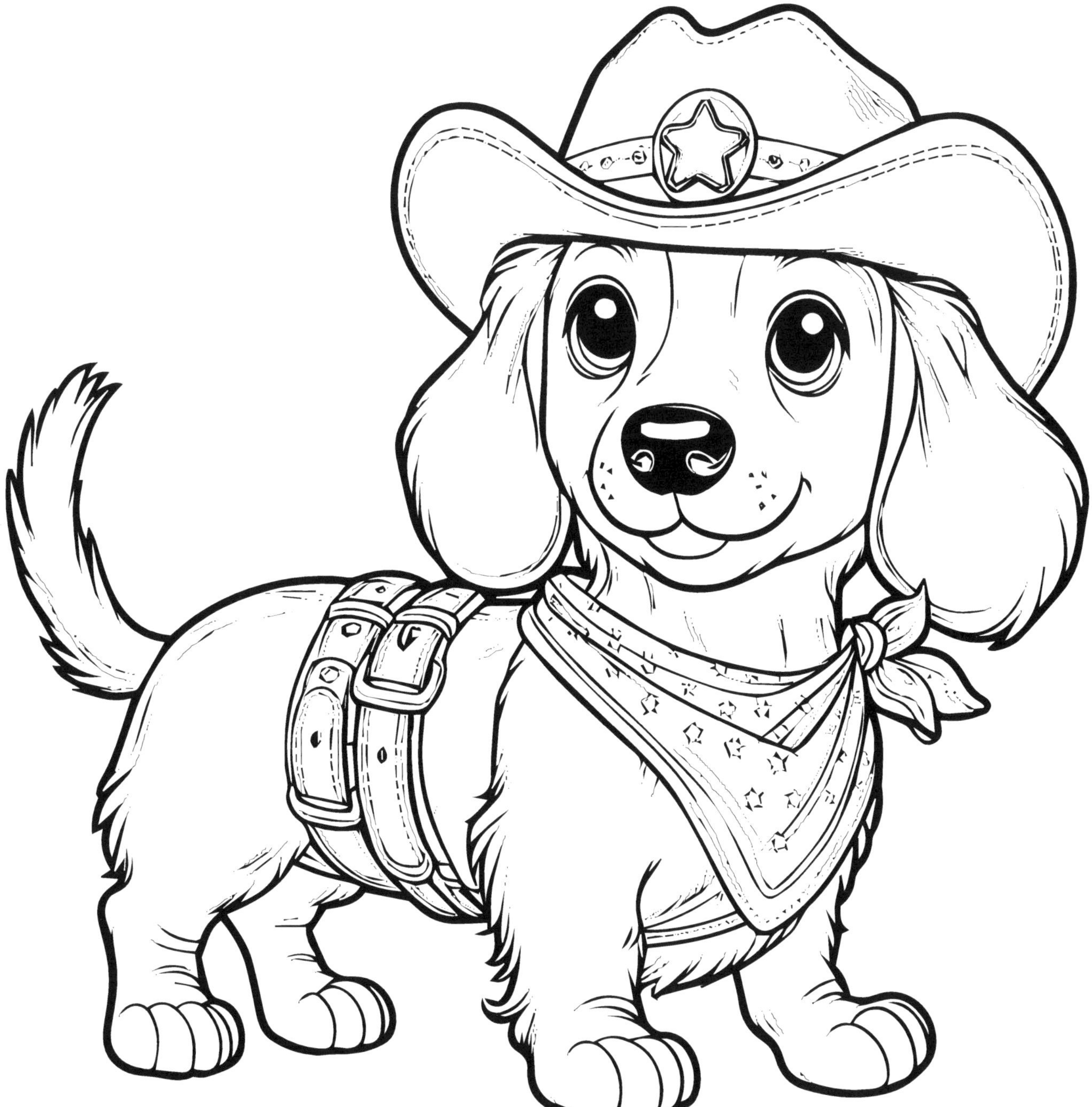

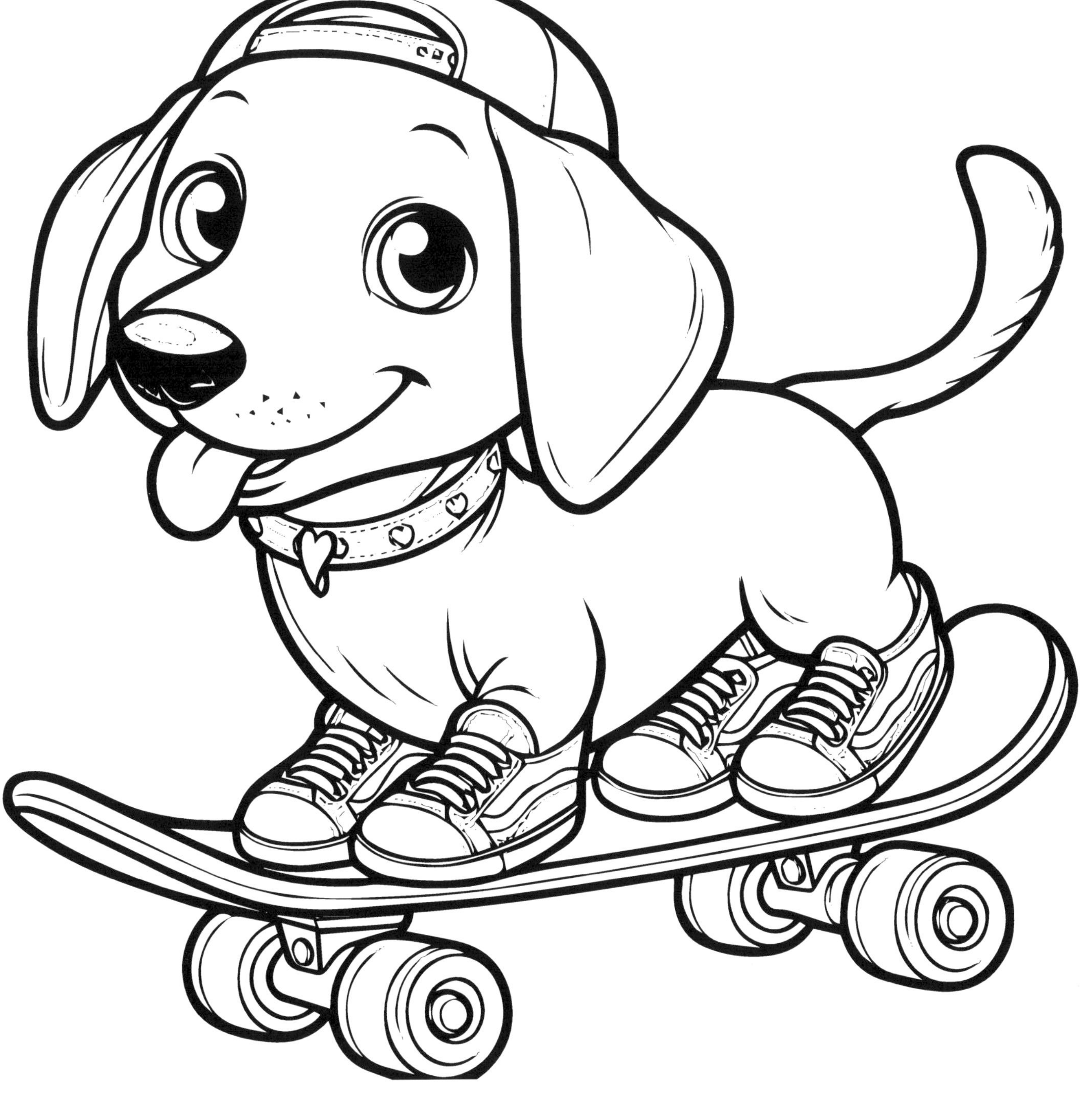

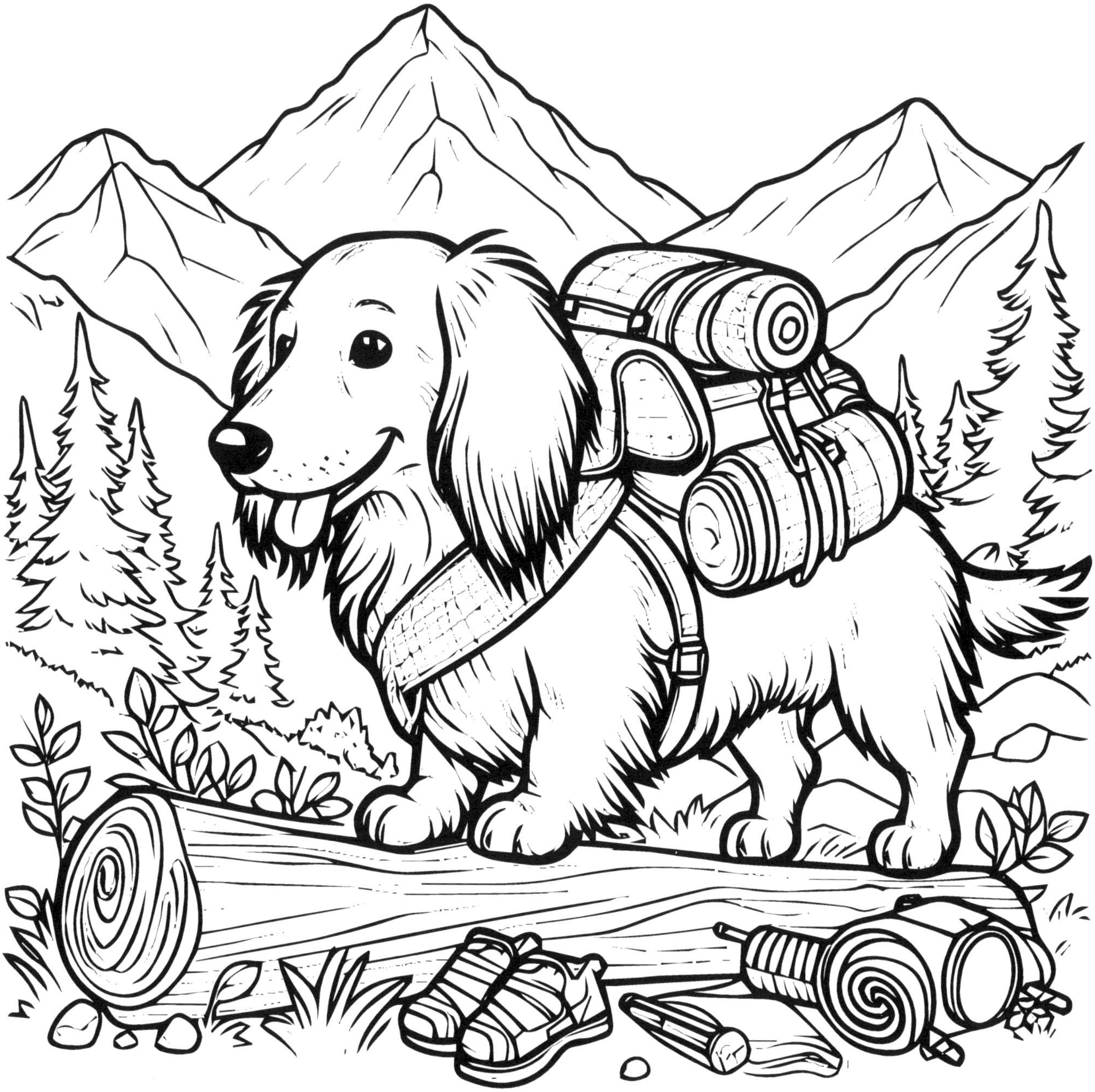

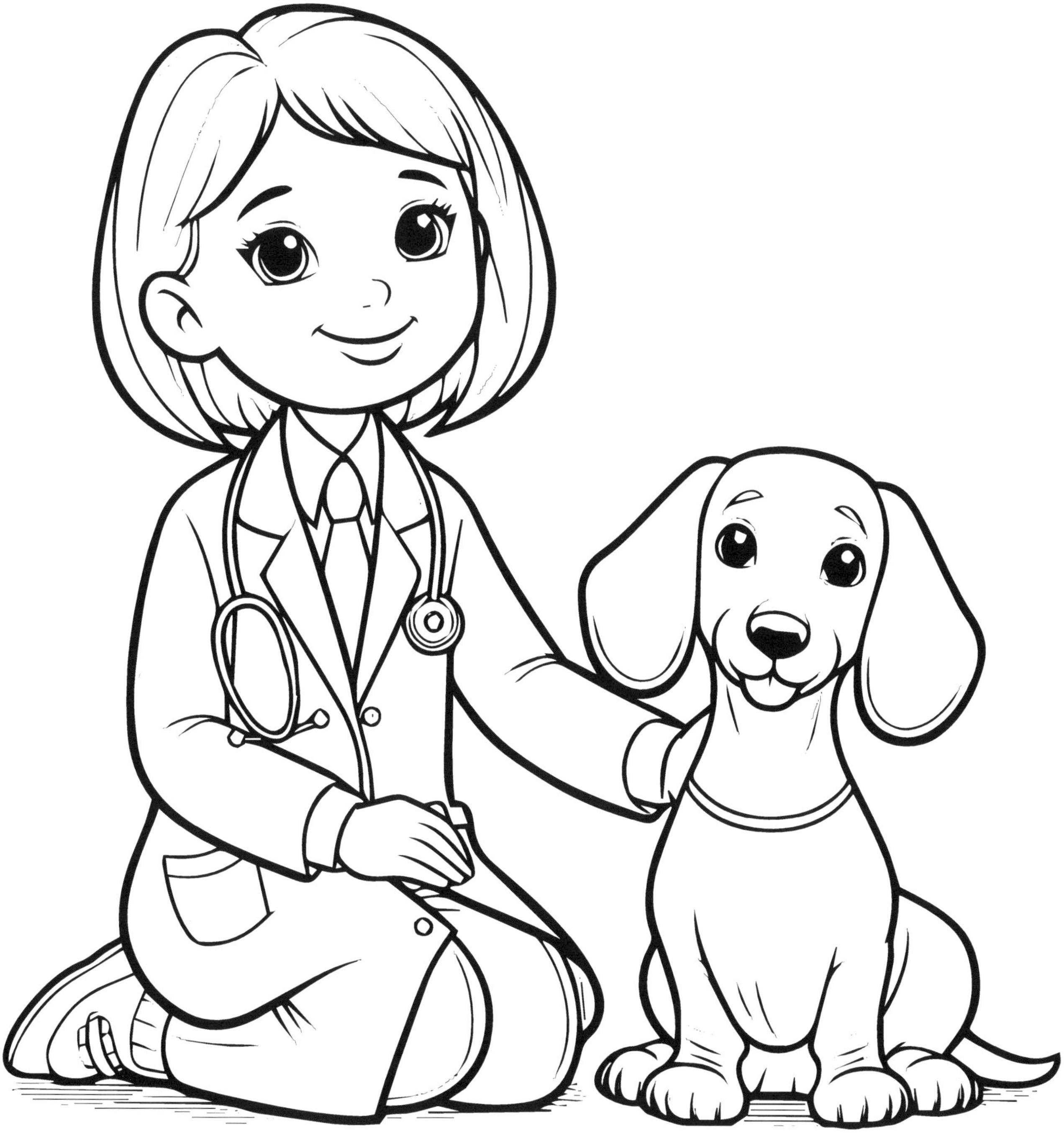

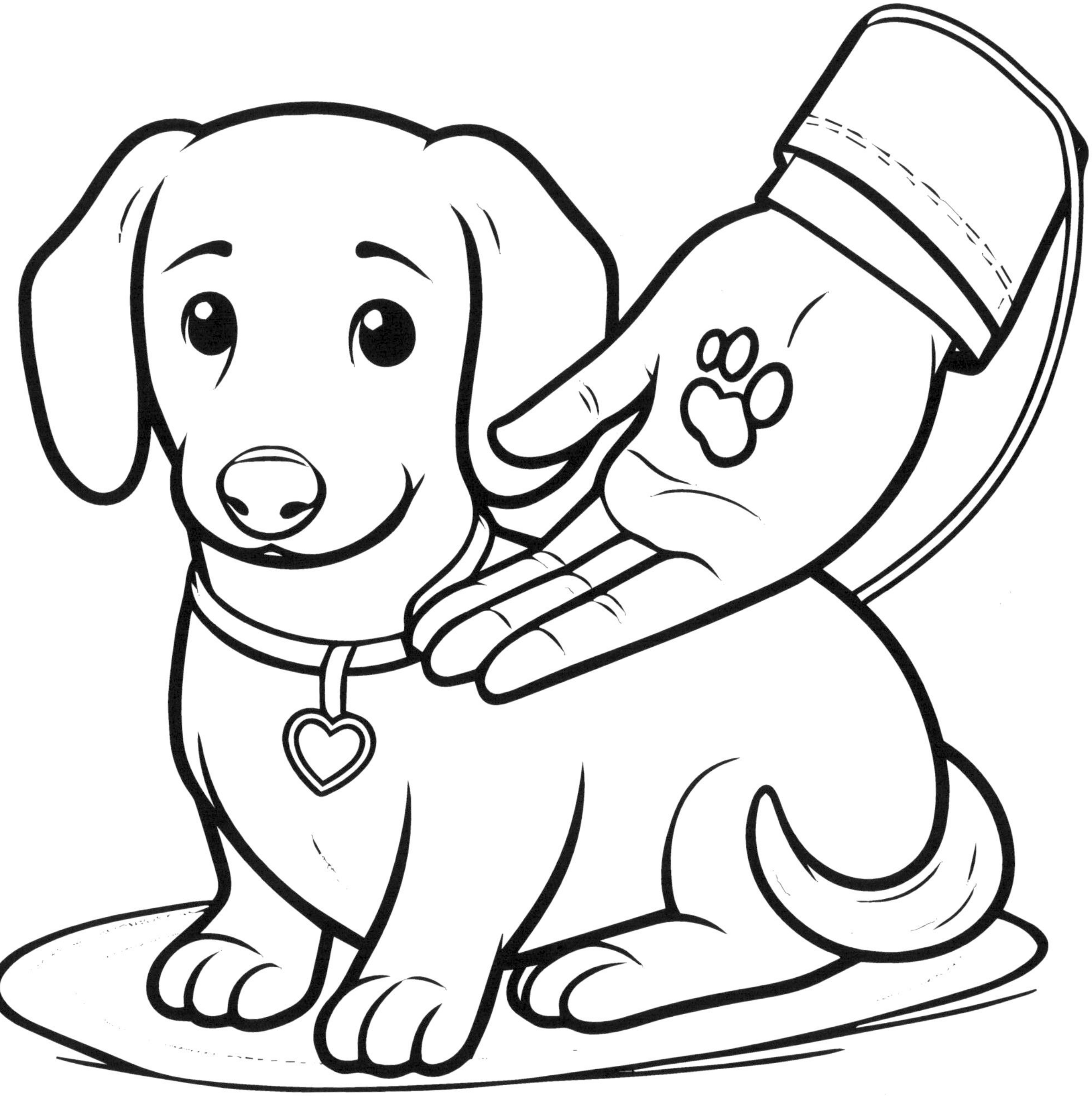

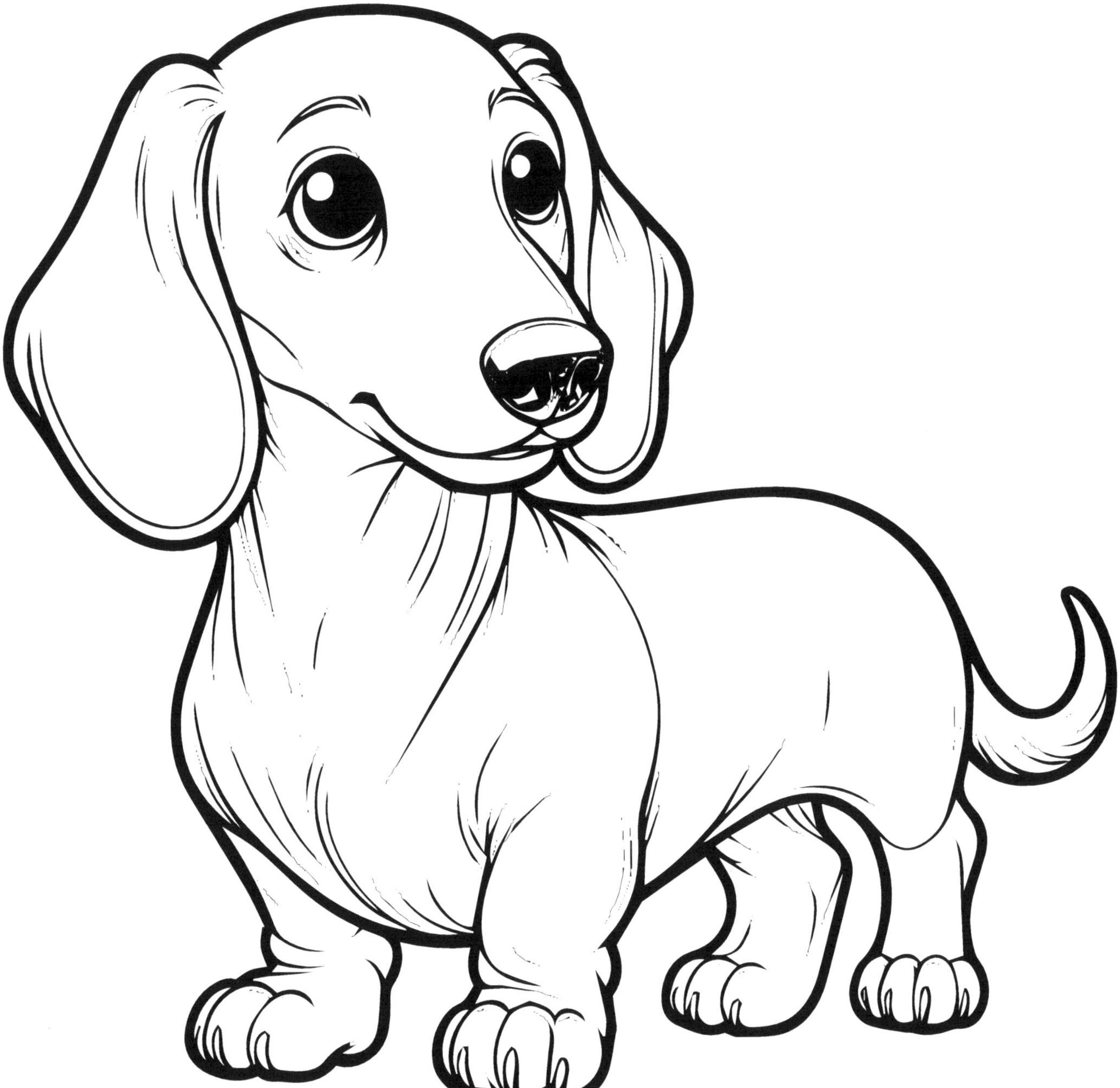

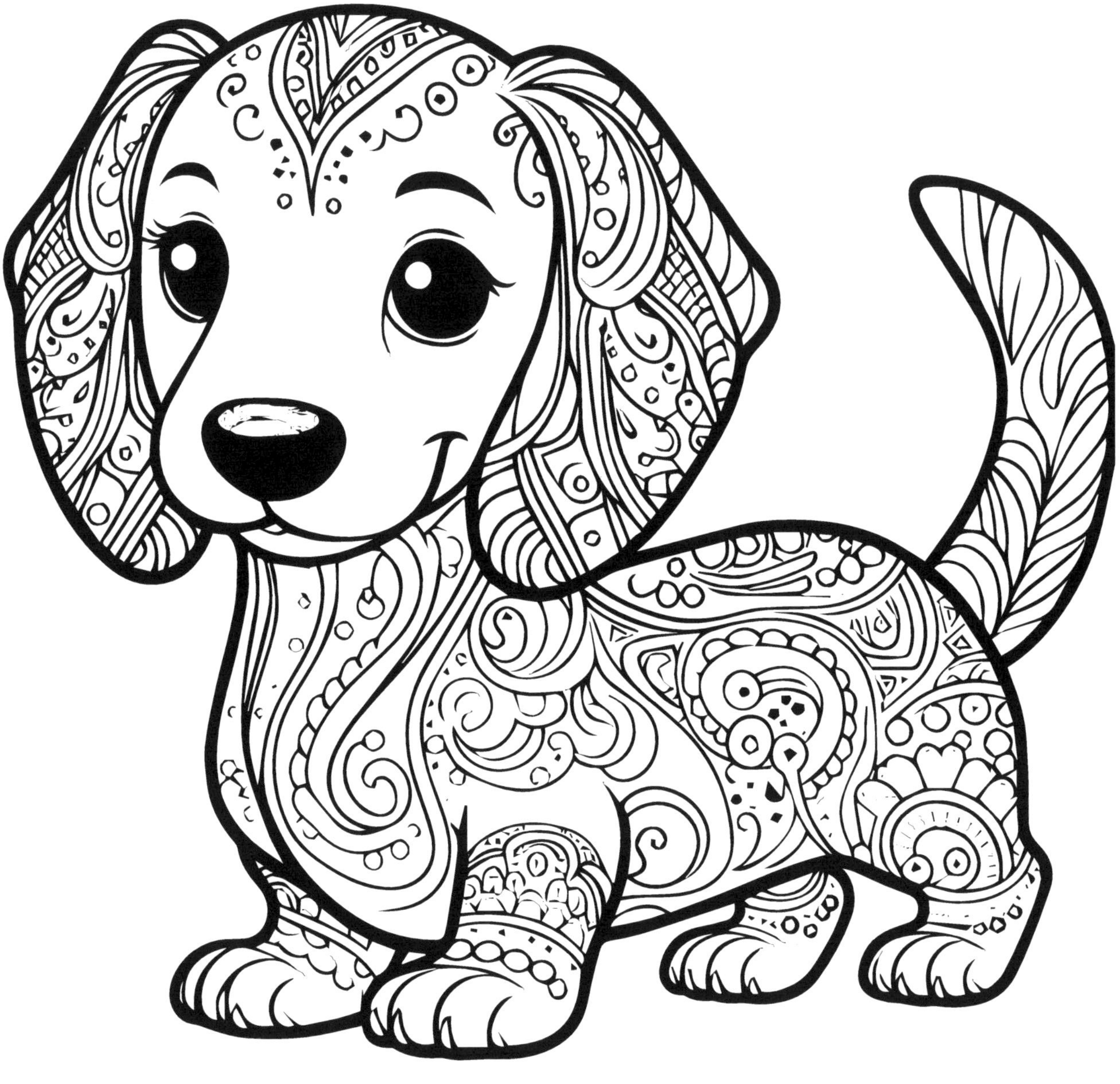

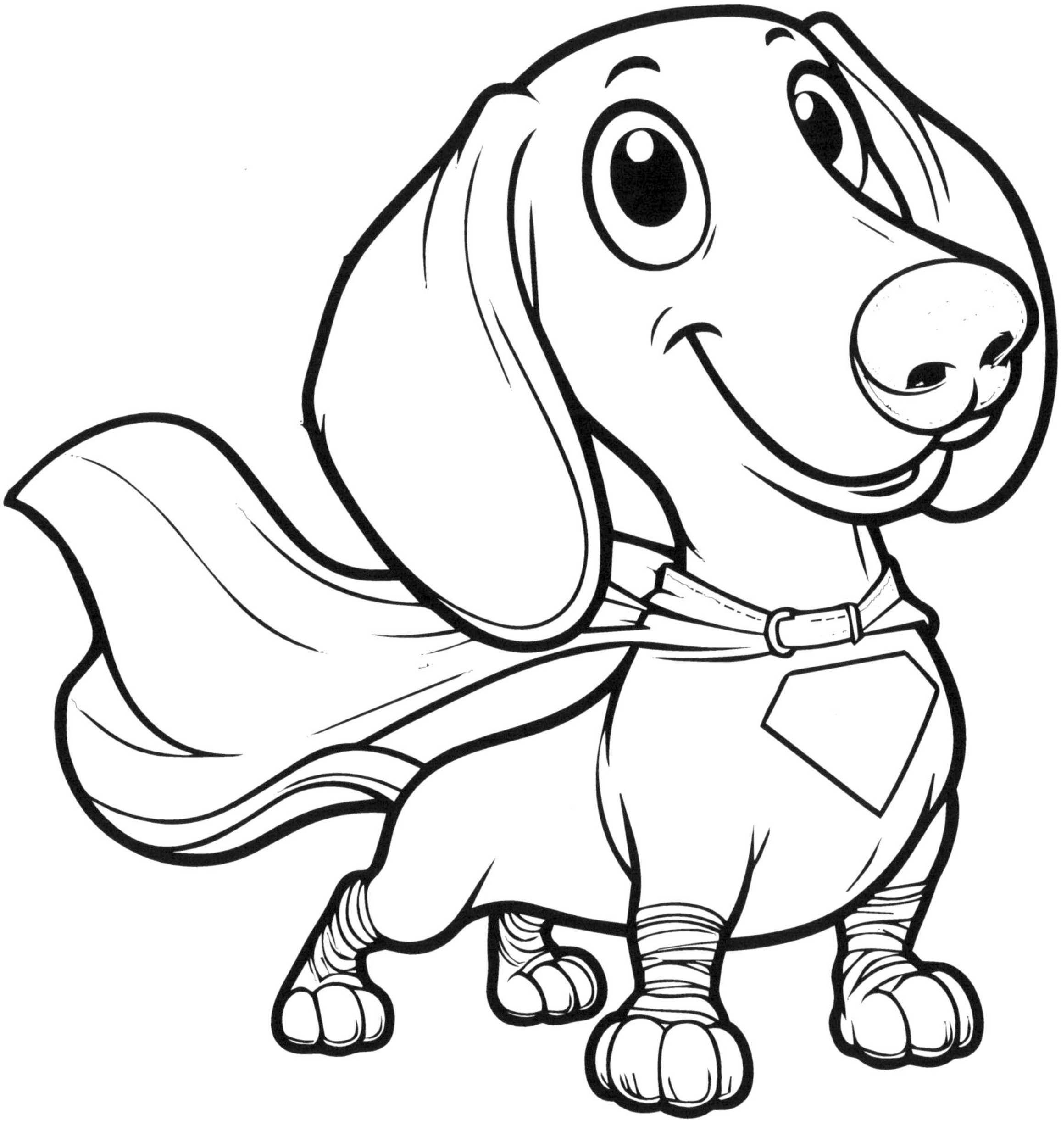

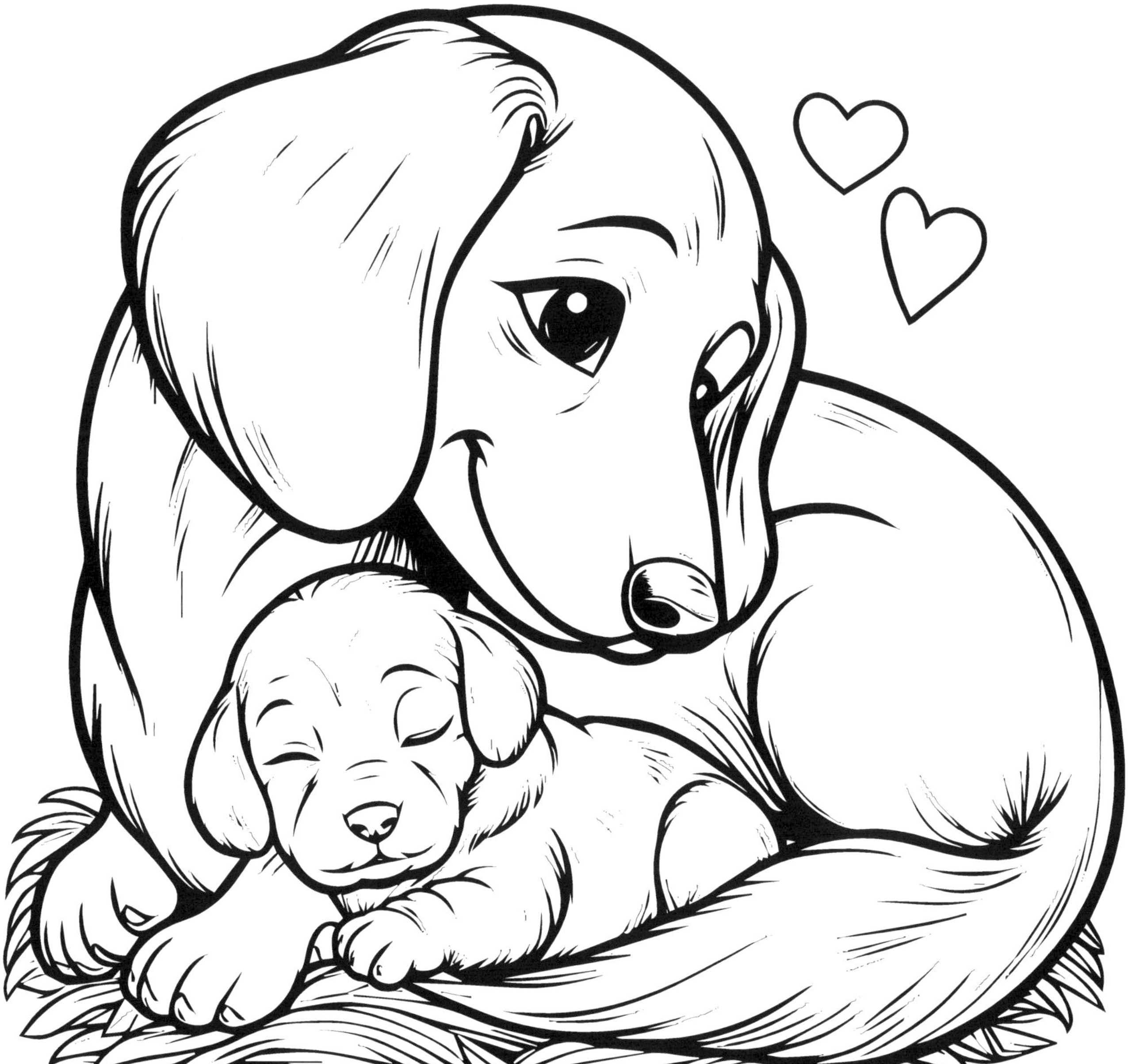

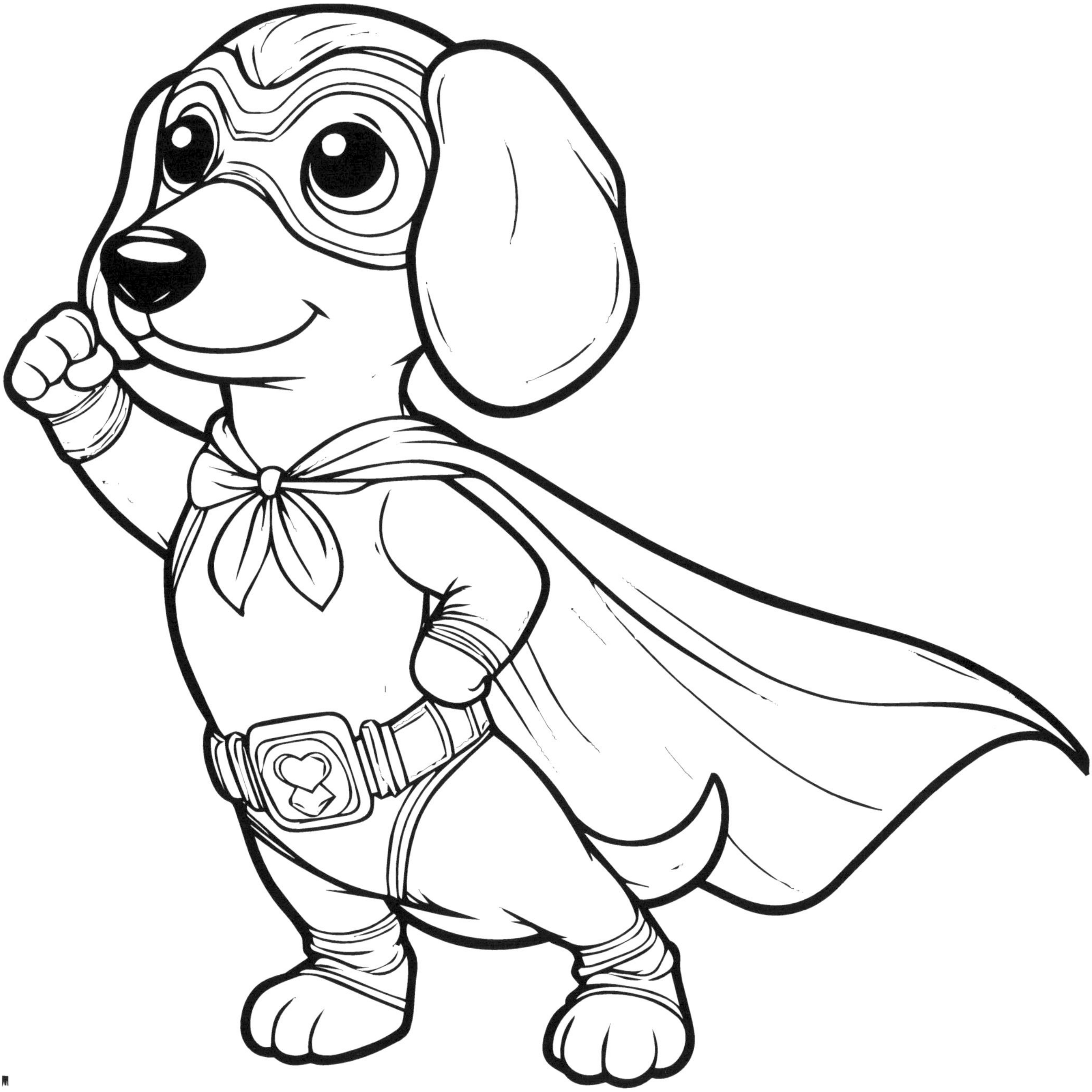

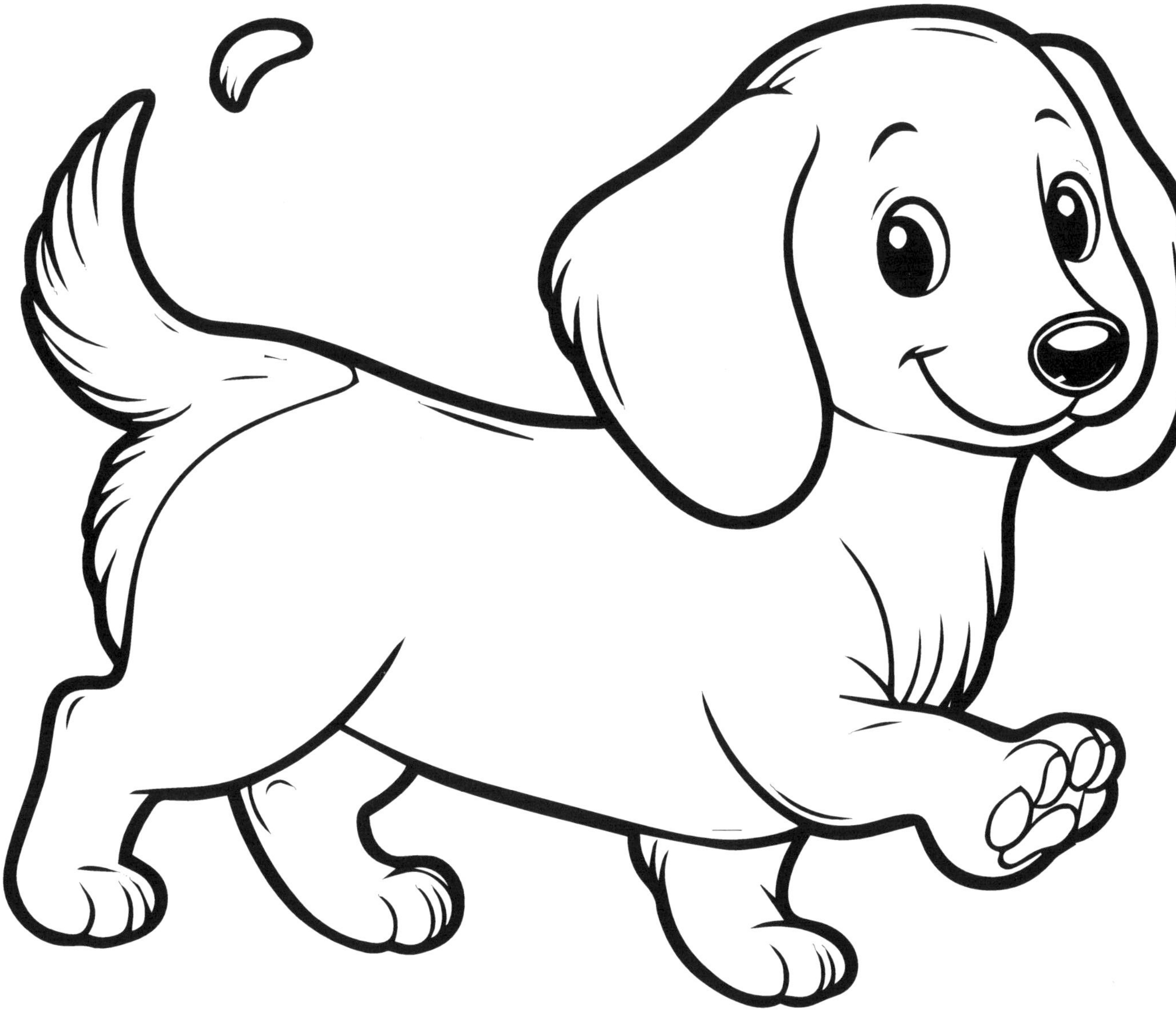

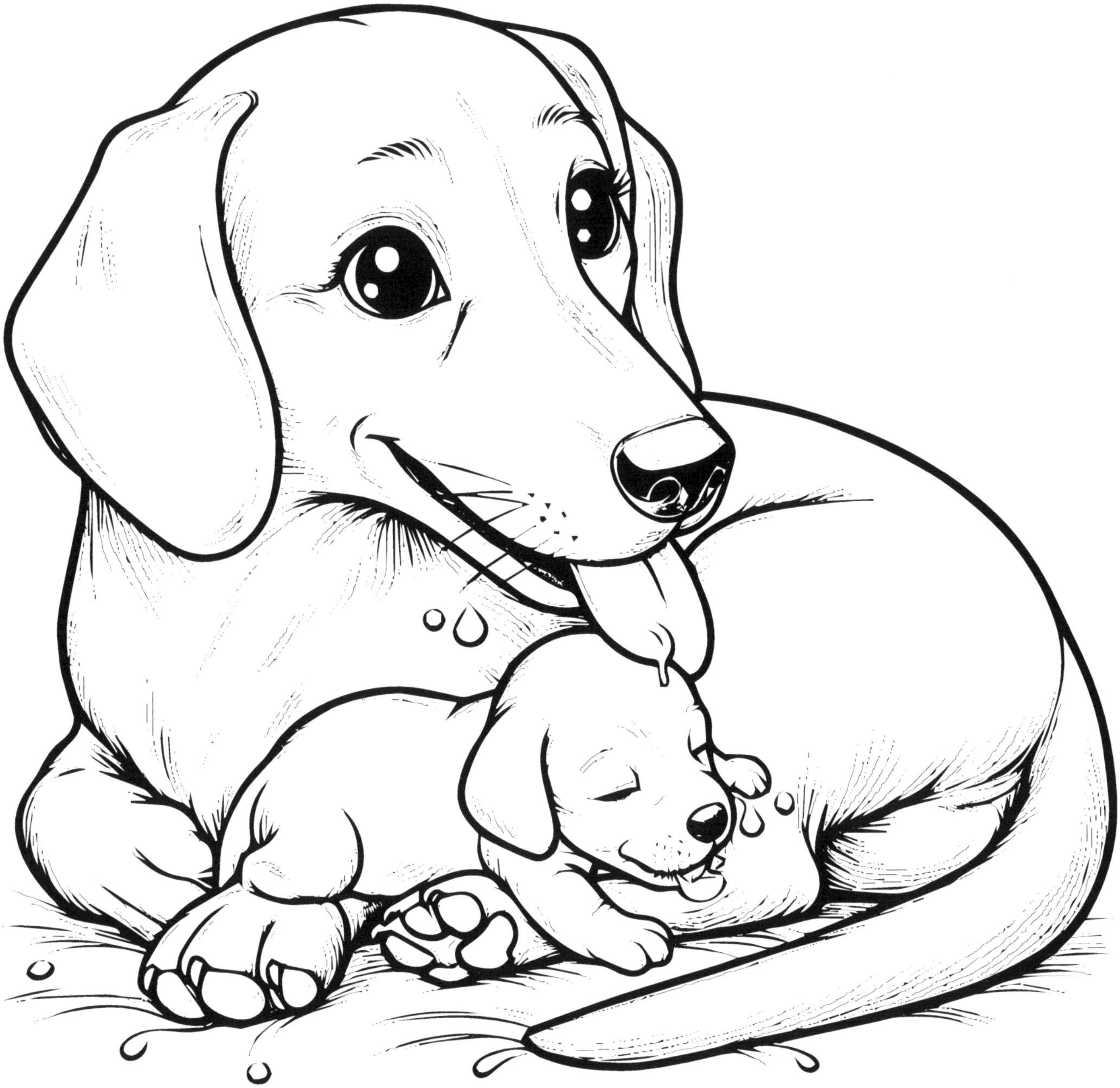

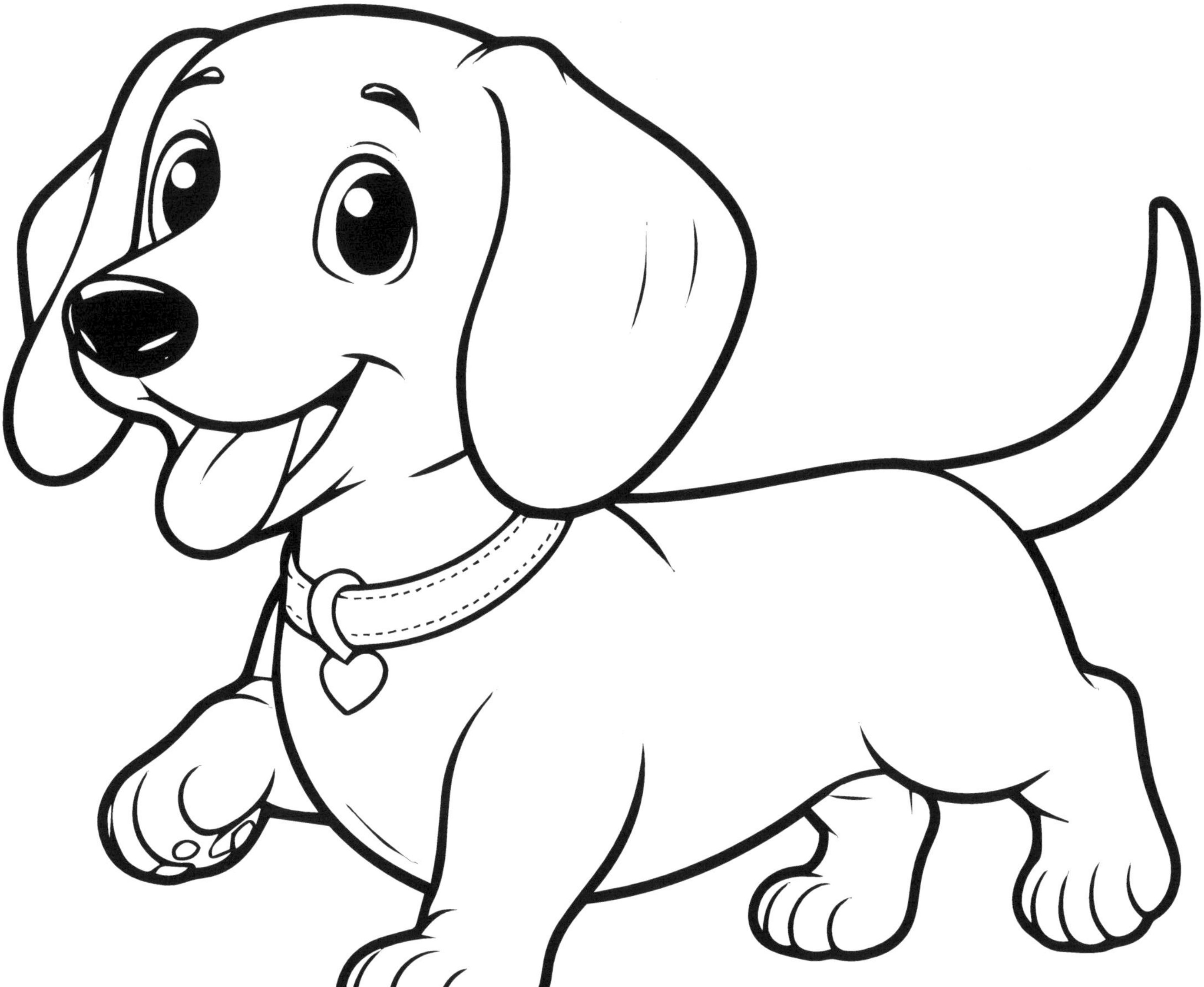

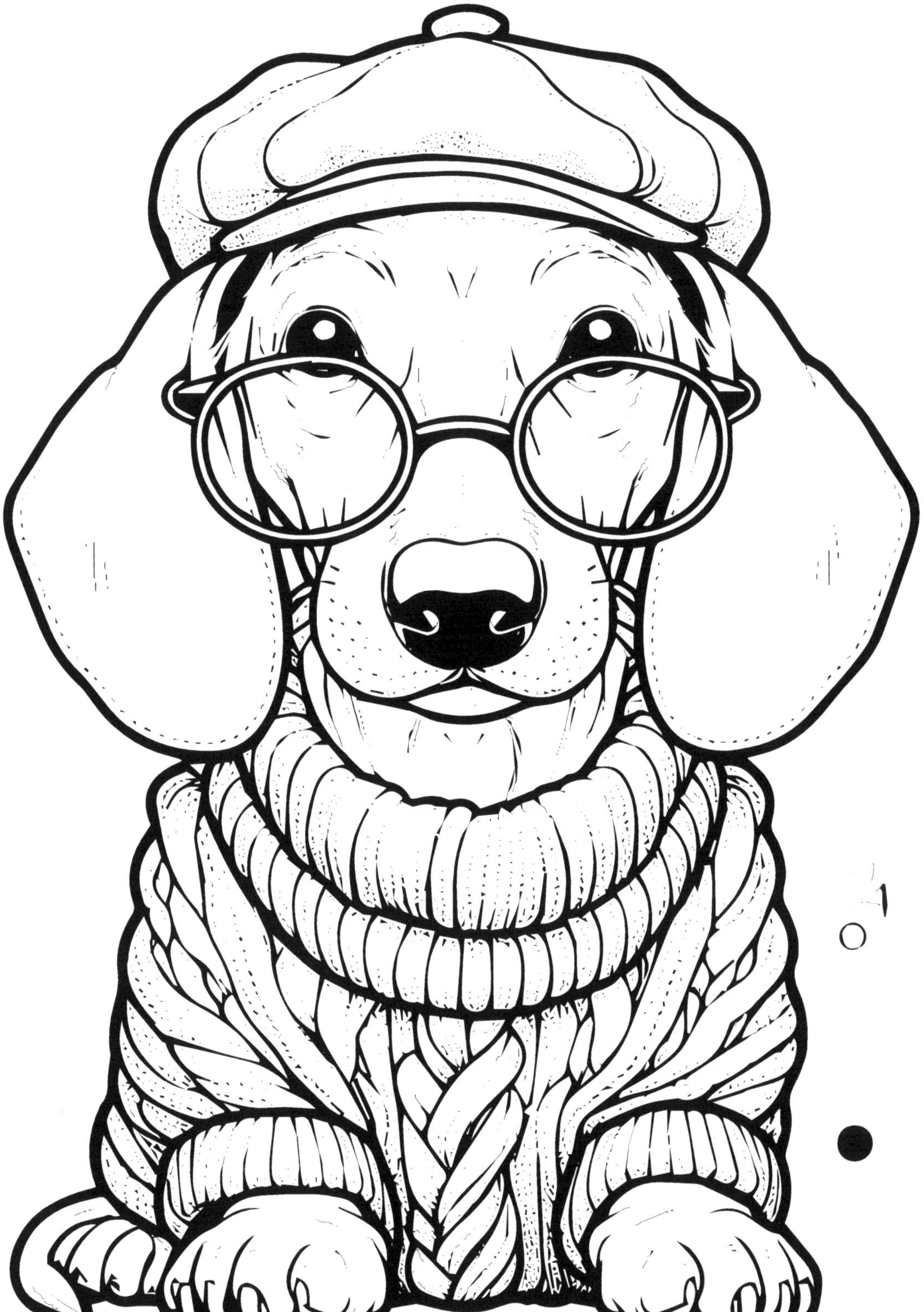

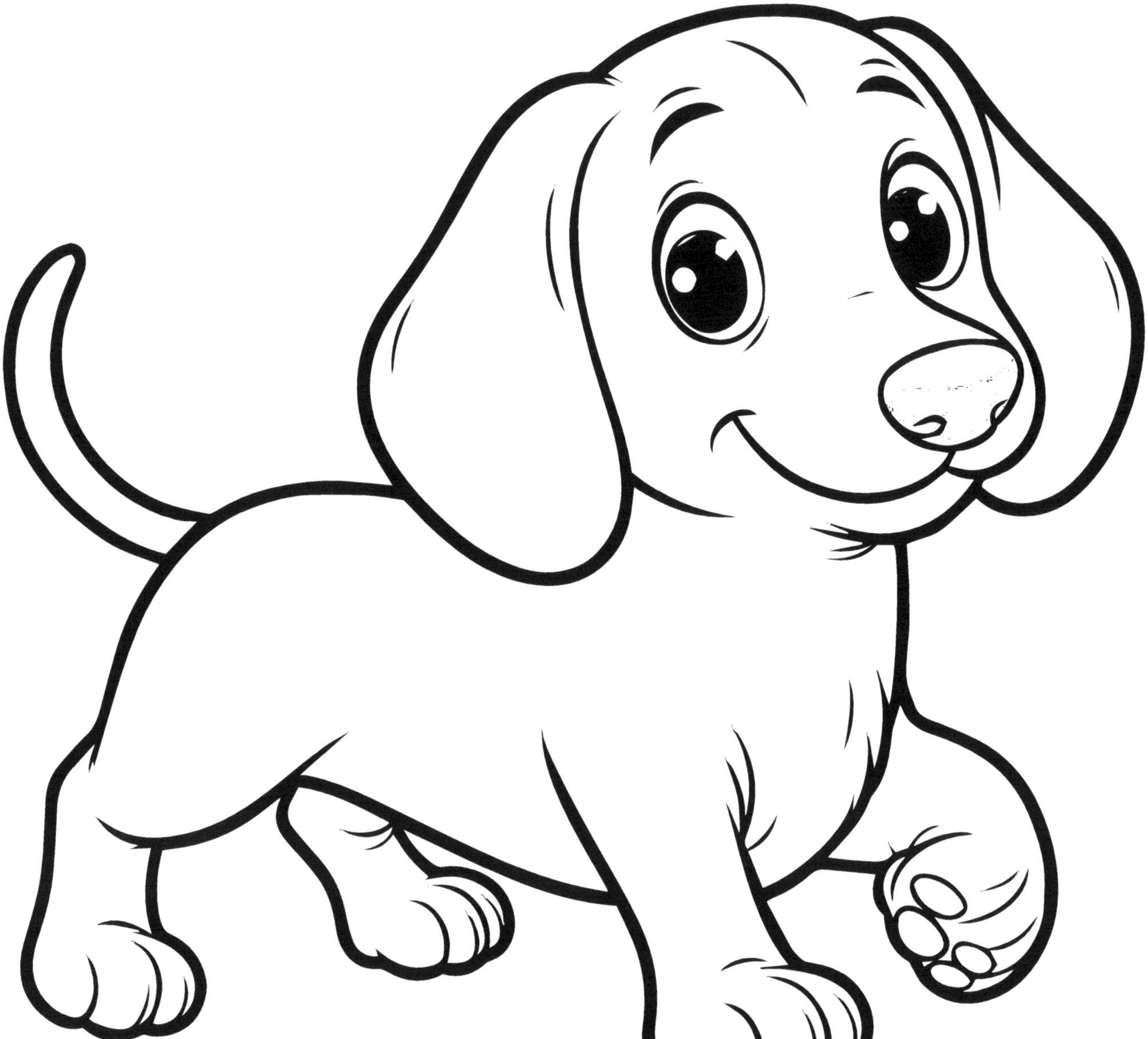

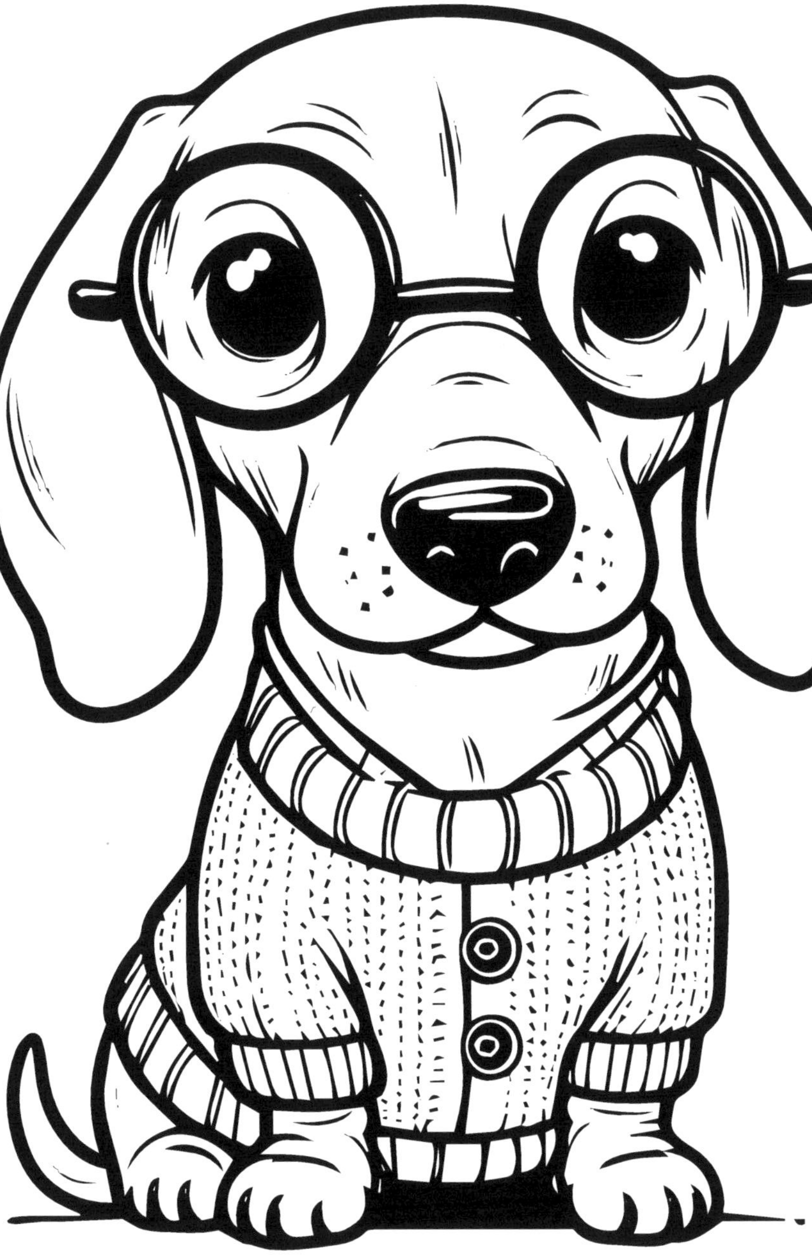

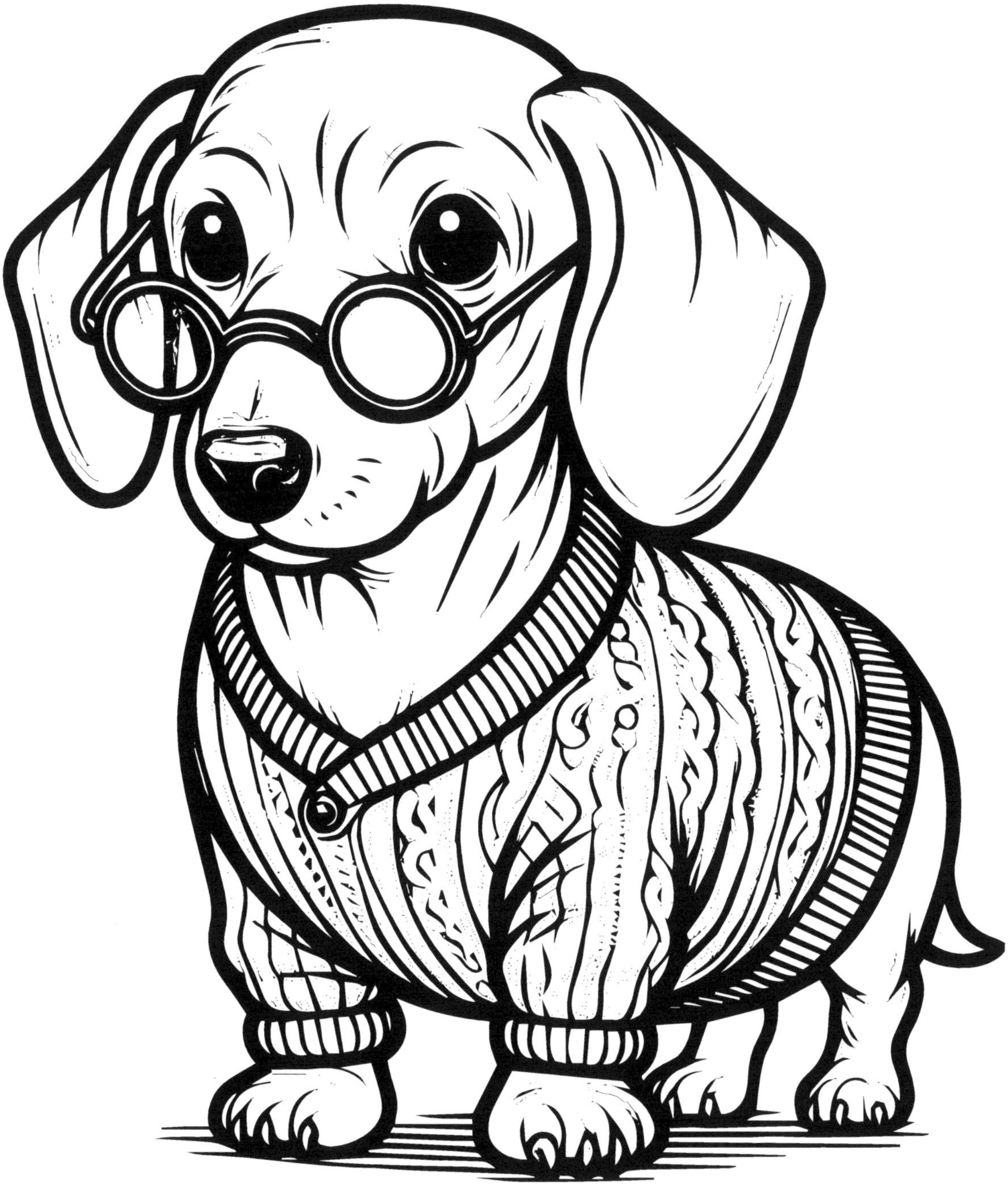

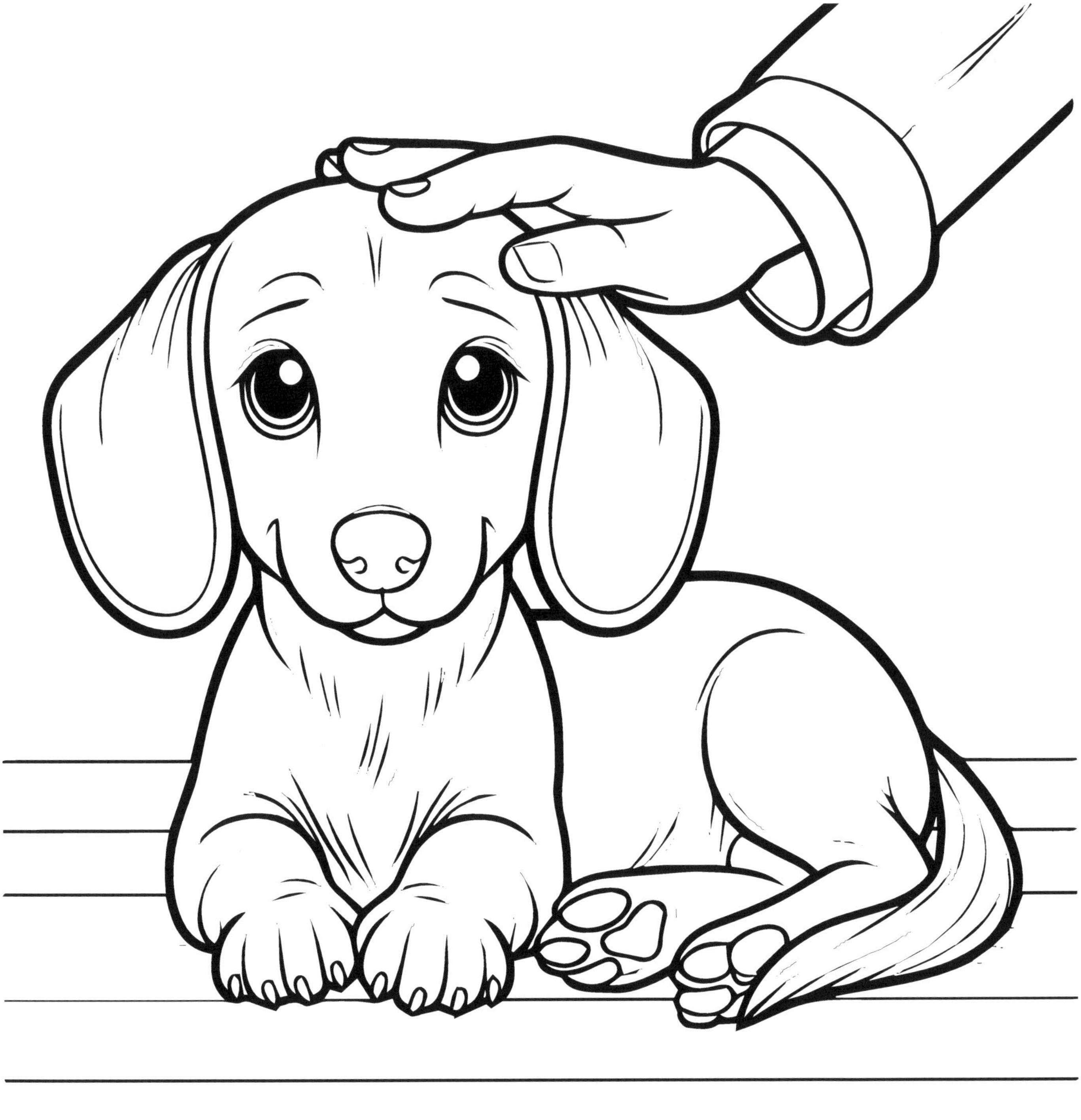

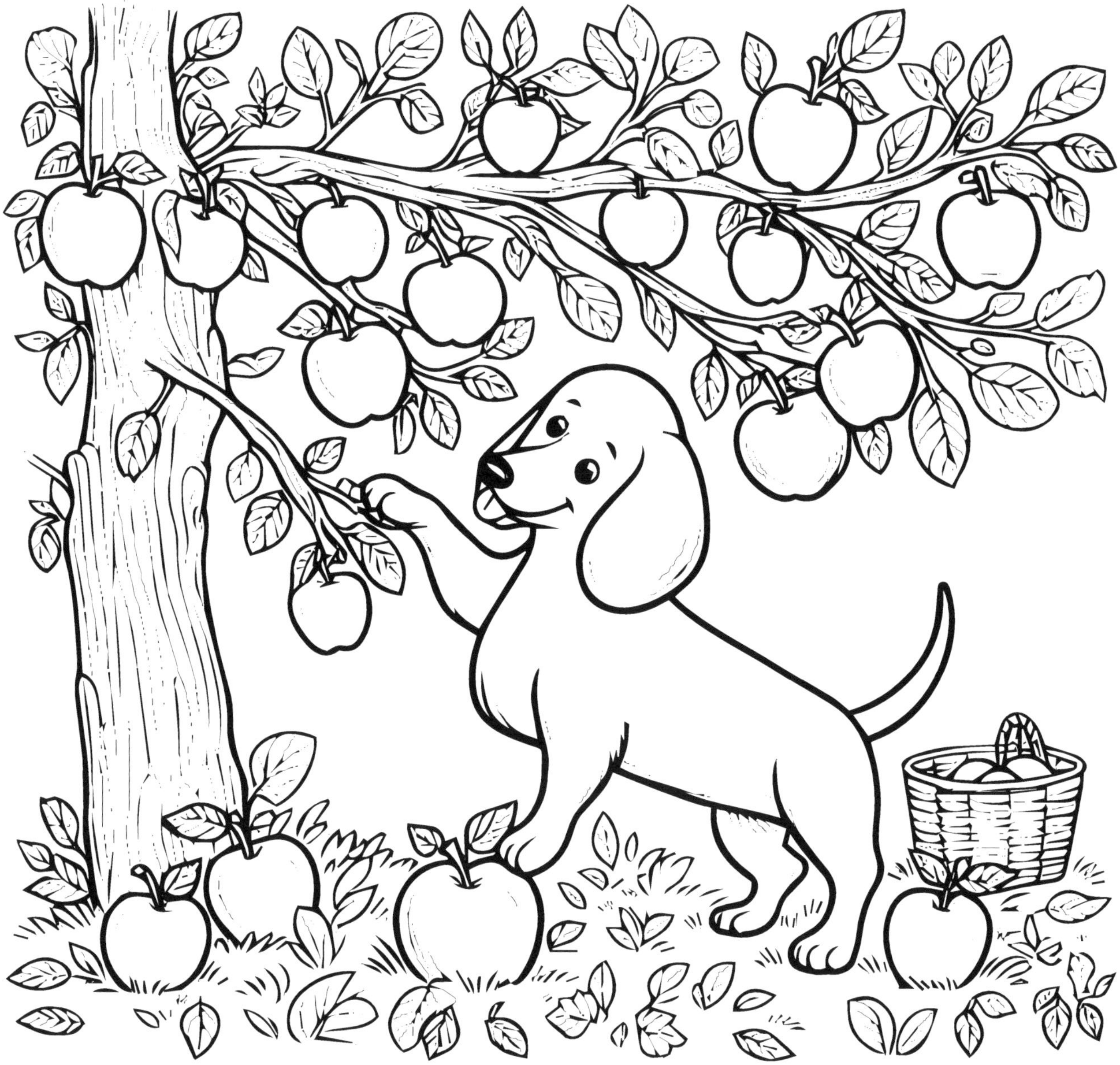

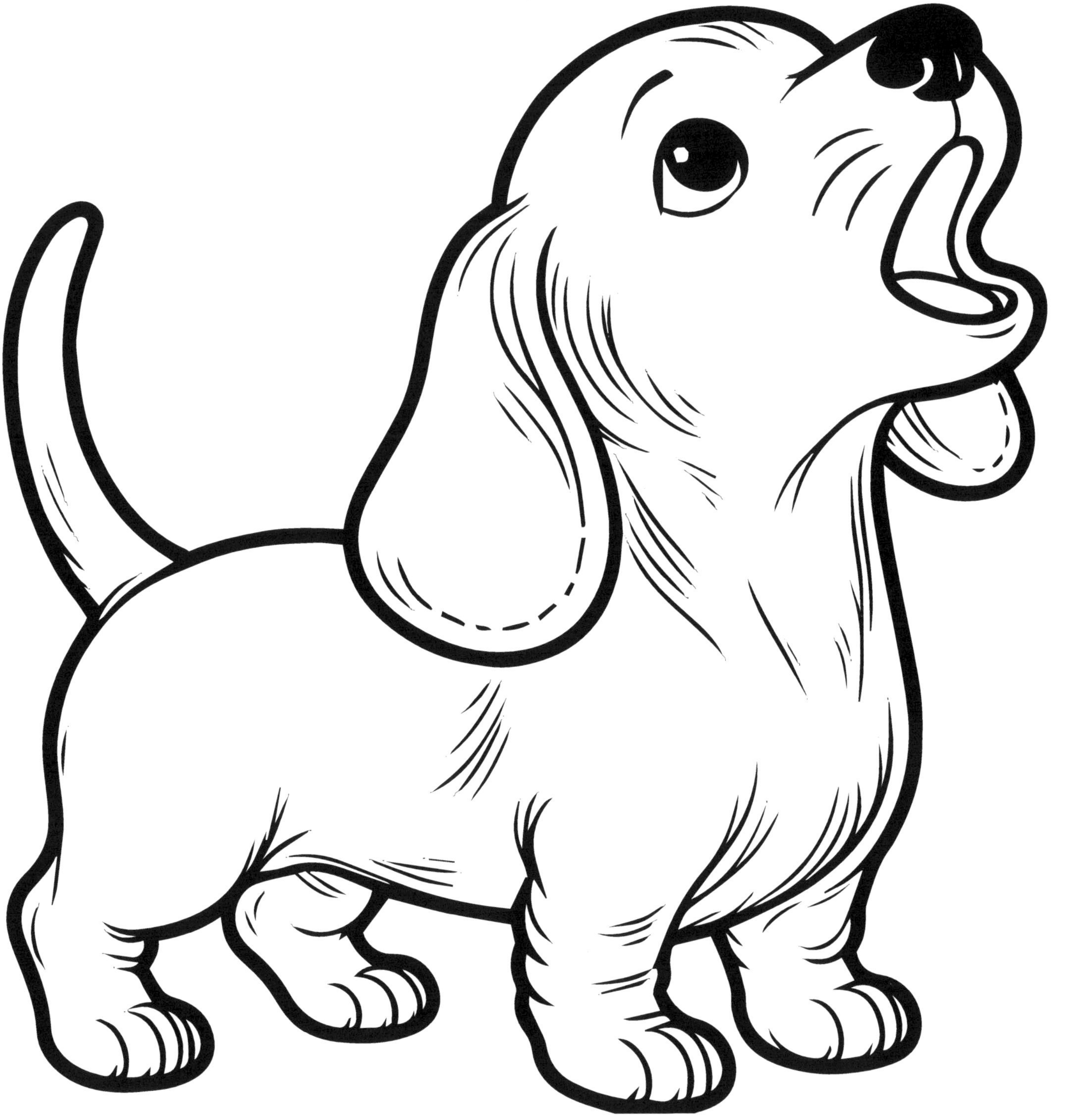

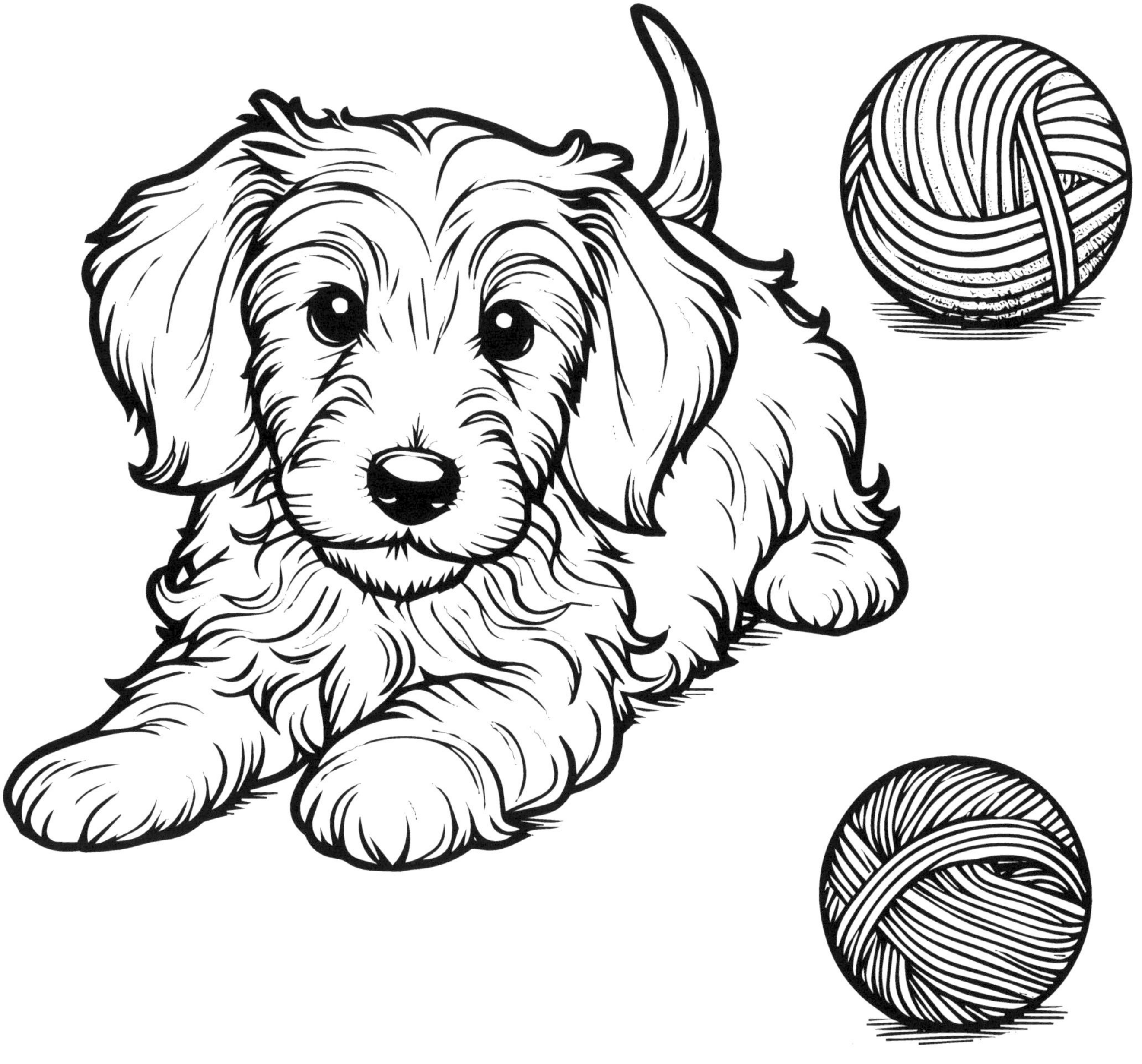

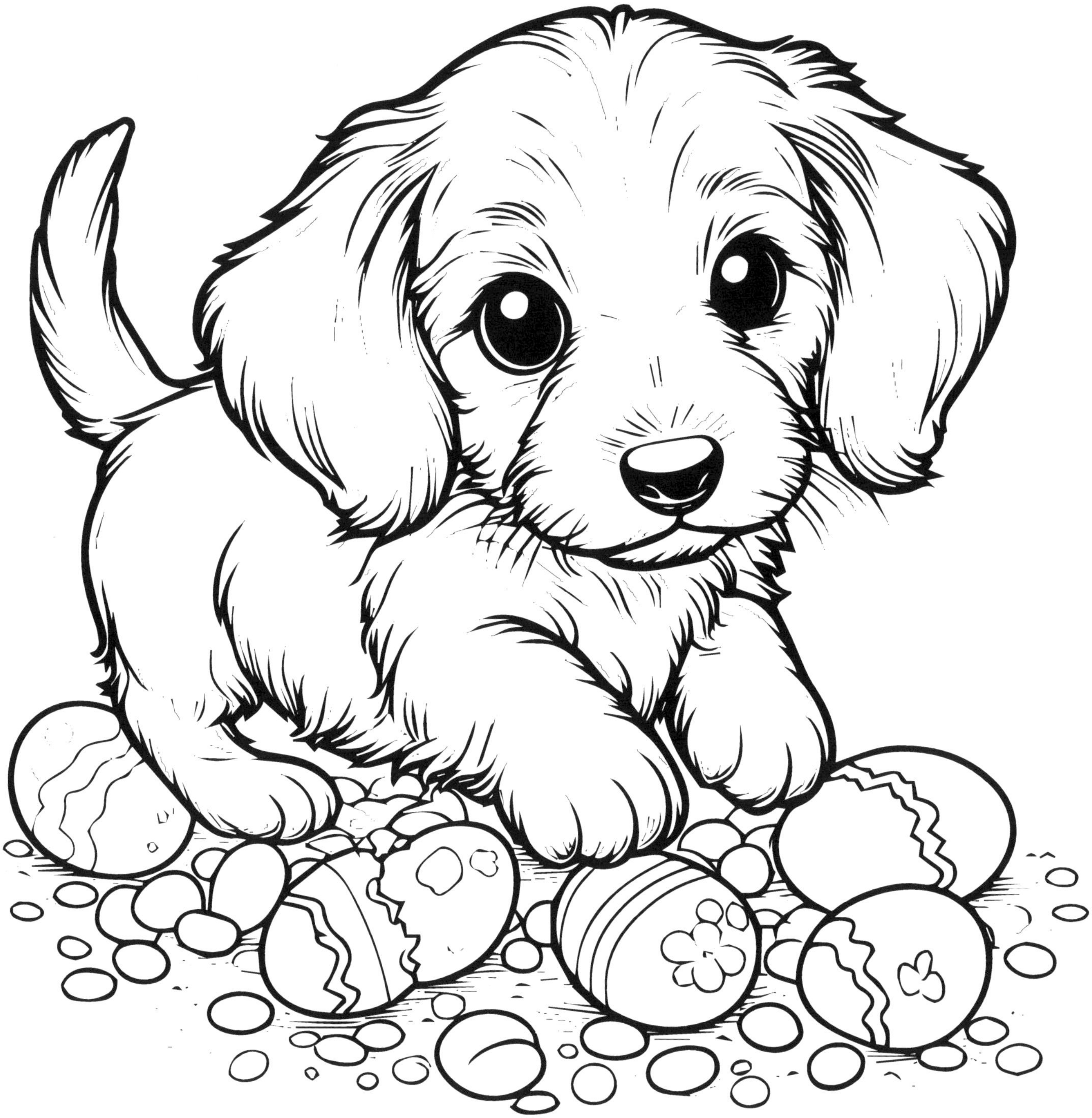

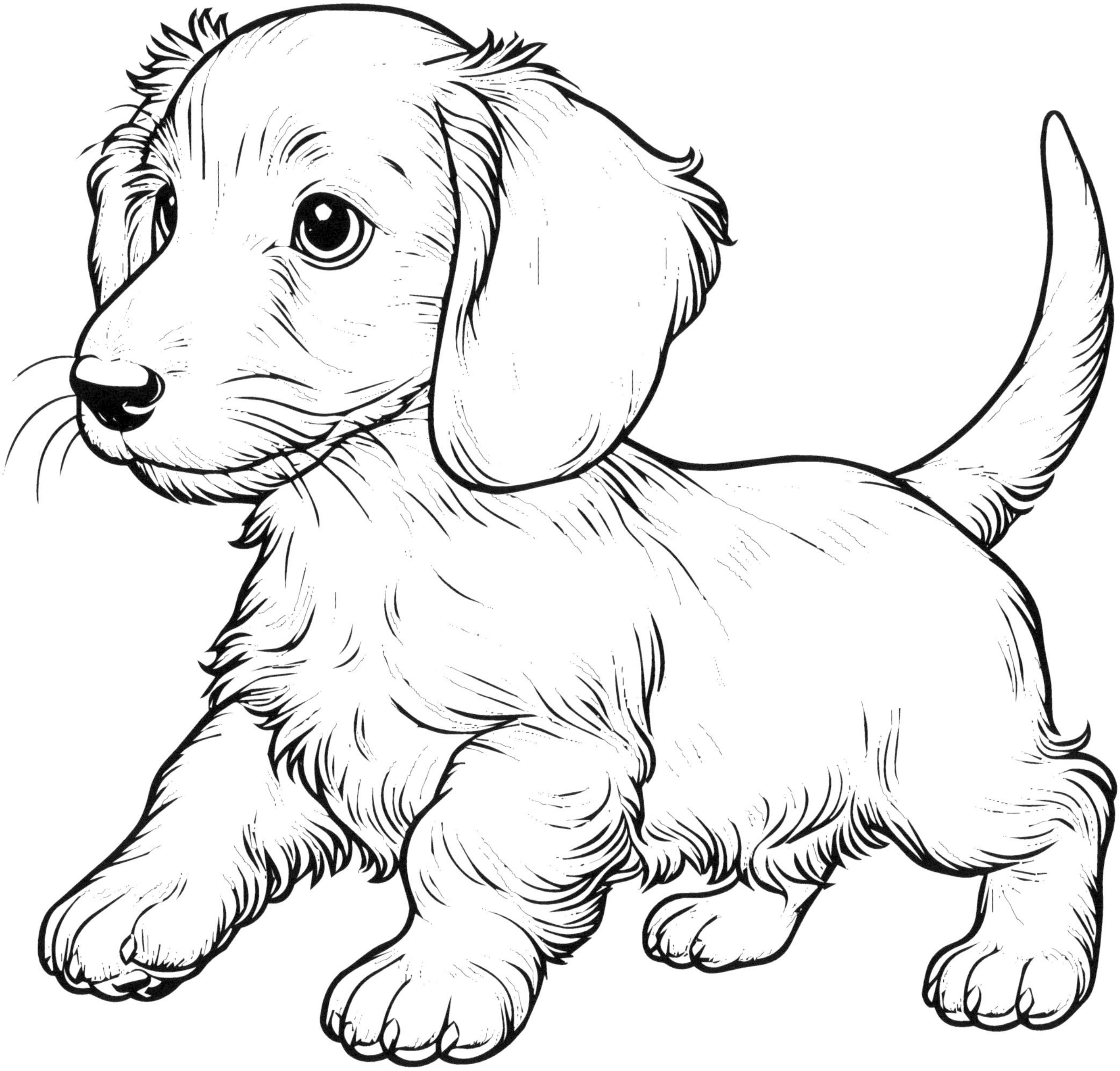

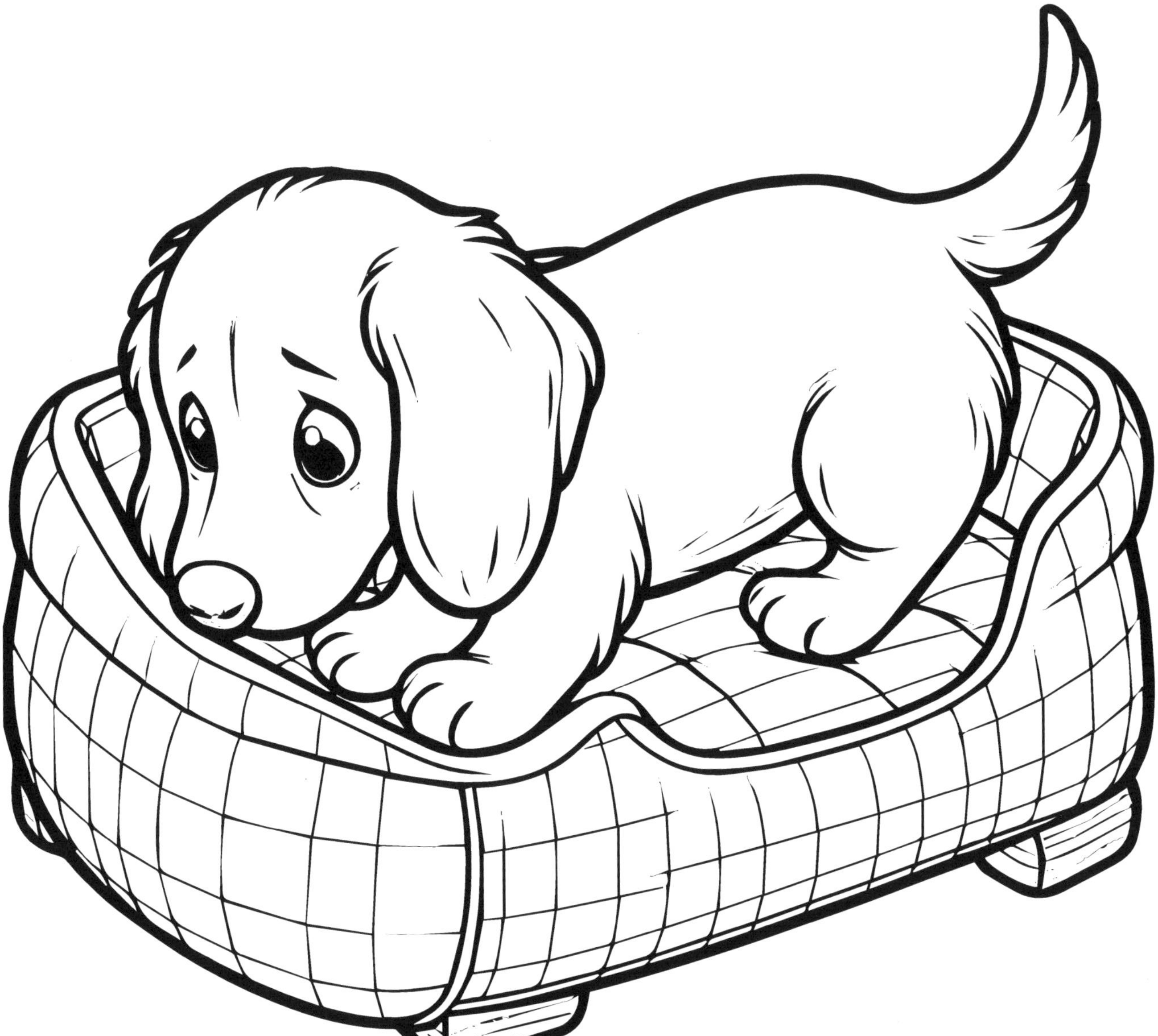

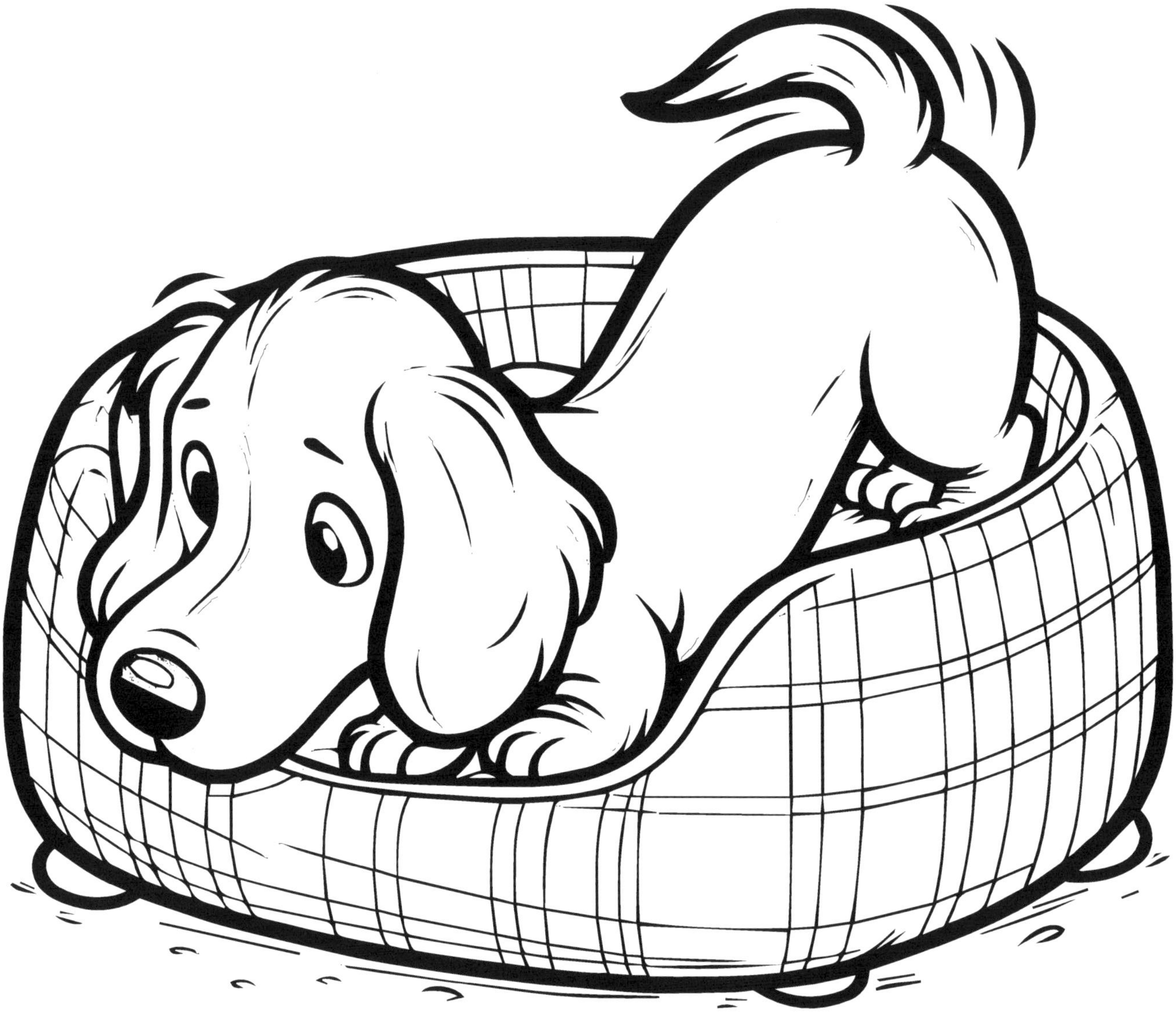

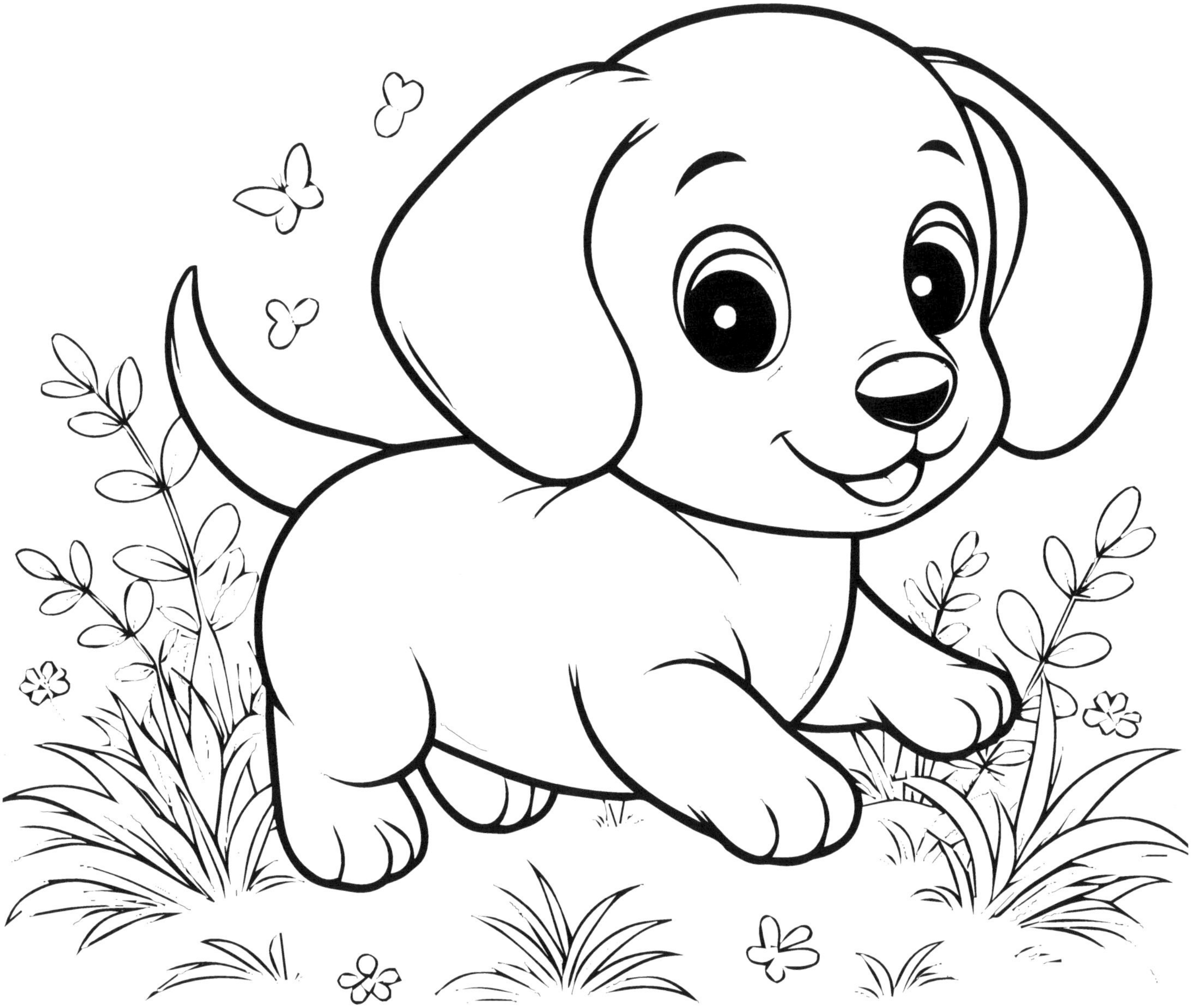

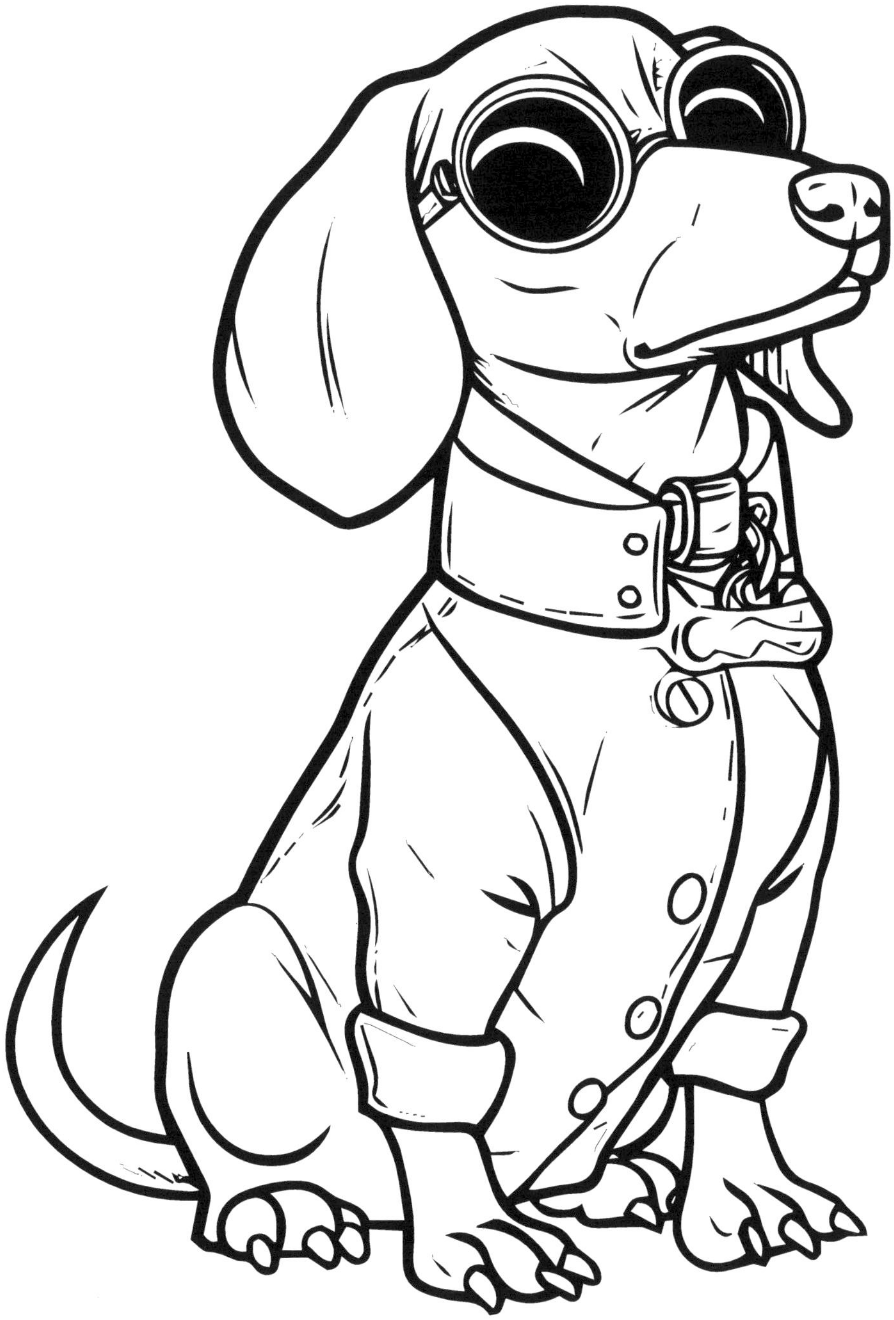

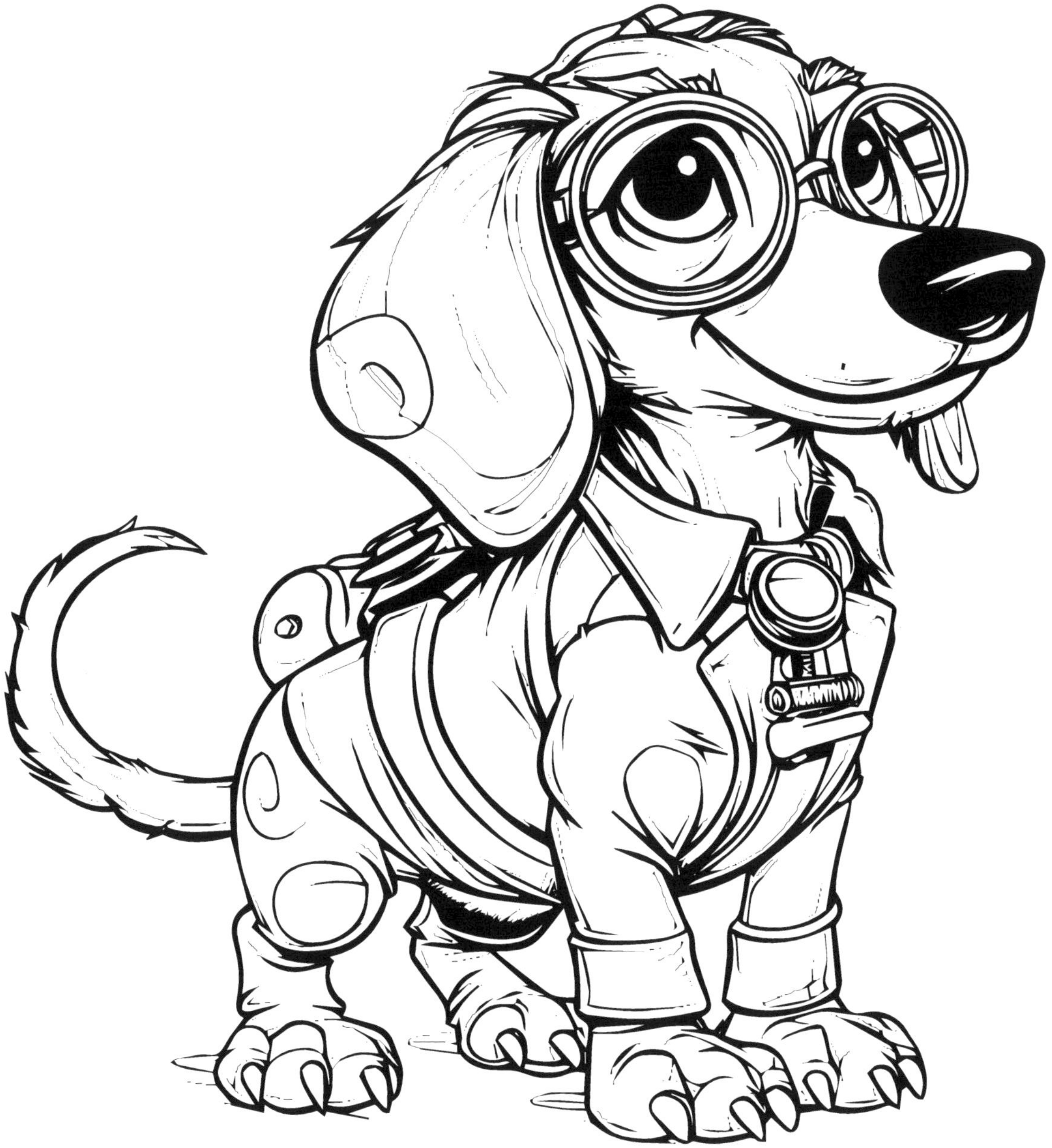

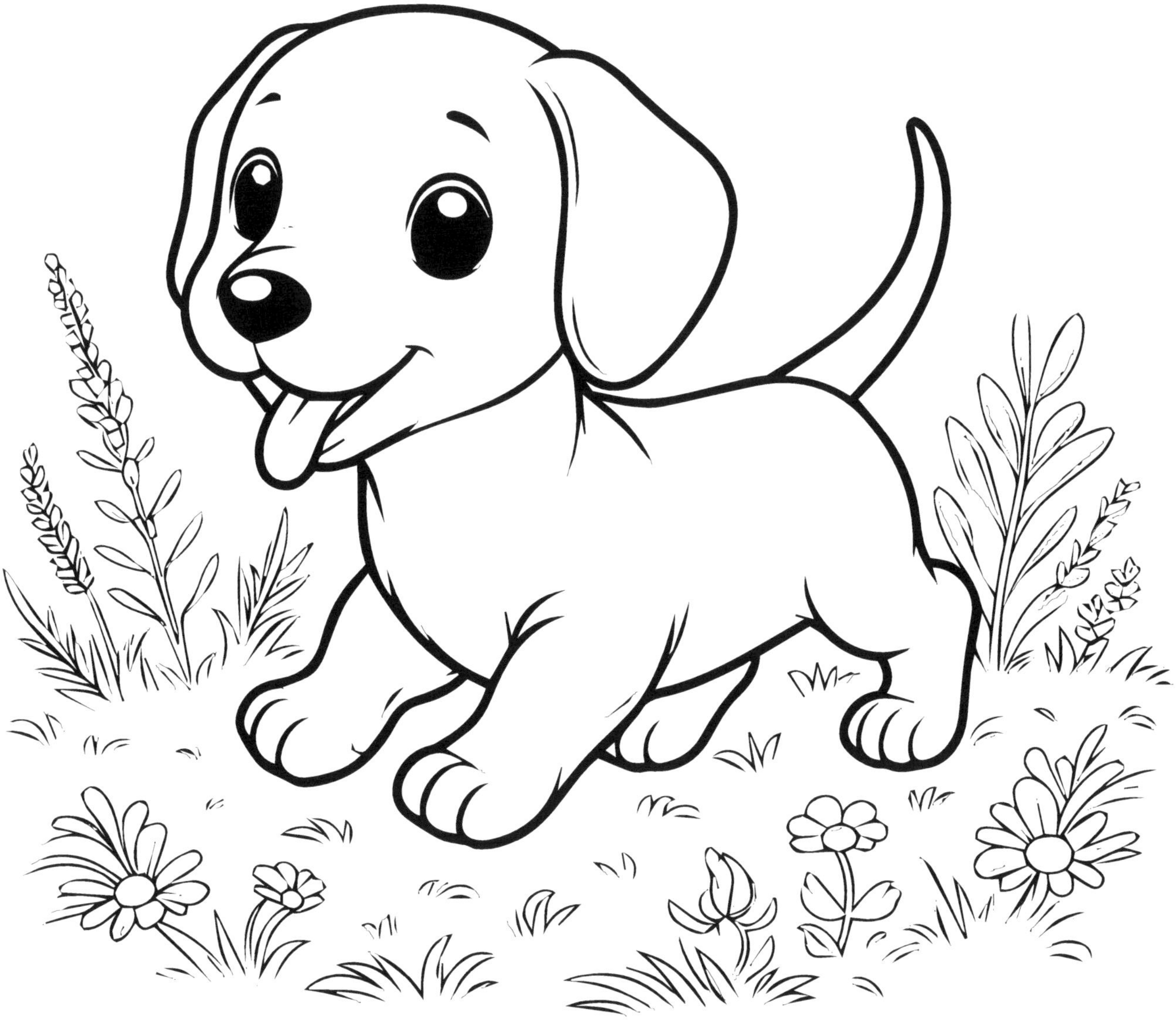

Made in the USA
Columbia, SC
05 January 2025

51219126R00057